AN OASIS OF DELIGHT

AN OASIS OF DELIGHT

The History of
The Birmingham Botanical Gardens

Phillada Ballard

Duckworth

First published in 1983 by
Gerald Duckworth & Co. Ltd.
The Old Piano Factory
43 Gloucester Crescent, London NW1

© 1983 by The Birmingham Botanical and
Horticultural Society

ISBN 0 7156 1776 1 (cased)

British Library Cataloguing in Publication Data

Ballard, Phillada
An oasis of delight: the history of the Birmingham
Botanical gardens since 1832.
  1. Birmingham Botanical Gardens – History
I. Title
580.'74'4 42496   QK73.G72B/

ISBN 0-7156-1776-1

Photoset in North Wales by
Derek Doyle & Associates, Mold, Clwyd
and printed in Great Britain by
The Alden Press, Oxford

Contents

Foreword

In this country there is a long and rewarding tradition of collaboration between professional and amateur botanists and horticulturalists. The sesquicentenary of the Birmingham Botanical and Horticultural Society is a proper occasion on which to celebrate these joint endeavours. The Birmingham Botanical Gardens, since their inception in 1832, have played a major role in botany and horticulture, and continue to flourish as an independent institution depending on local enthusiasm and interest.

It is true that at times relations between botany and horticulture have been strained when botanists, following the strict interpretation of the international rules of botanical nomenclature or applying the results of their taxonomic investigations, require the provoking replacement of well-known plant names with less familiar ones. None the less the bond between the two sciences remains firm and mutually beneficial.

The Gardens, which celebrated their 150th anniversary last year, have a splendid record of achievement as this book affirms, and the author, Mrs Ballard, has certainly provided a fascinating account of the interwoven threads of all their activities and of the chronicle of events which have led to their present renown. It is fortunate that the author is a professsional historian with wide interests in horticulture and botany.

The original plans for the Garden were prepared by the formidable Scot, John Claudius Loudon, who was born exactly 200 years ago and whose wife was a native of Birmingham. Changes have certainly occurred over the last century, but many of Loudon's features are still to be seen in the Gardens.

I value the opportunity to congratulate the Society on its praiseworthy history and to commend this volume warmly as a valuable and most readable additional chapter of horticultural literature.

Sir George Taylor, D.Sc., F.R.S., LL.D., F.R.S.E., F.L.S., V.M.H. (Director of The Royal Botanic Gardens, Kew, 1956-1971).

Colour Plates

Acknowledgments

I am indebted to many people for their help in writing this book. In particular I should like to thank Miss V.E. Davis for invaluable assistance in researching some of the detail and for compiling the list of Presidents, Chairmen and Curators of the B.B.H.S. Professor J.G. Hawkes and Professor Donald Skelding gave me much valuable guidance on the botanical and horticultural aspects, while Chris Brickell, Director, and Peter Barnes, botanist, of The Royal Horticultural Society's Gardens at Wisley, kindly checked the synonymy.

In addition many people, both present and former employees of the B.B.H.S. and Committee members, provided valuable information on the Gardens, and I should especially like to thank Hugh and Anne Kenrick, Michael Worley, Leslie Godfrey, Philip Butler, Len Salt, Albert Williams, David Earp, Betty Carless, Dr Richard Lester, David Higgs and Louise Hall.

I am grateful to the people who took the trouble to write to me with their own personal memories and impressions of the Gardens over the years, especially Mr and Mrs A.D. Cook, Mrs Anne Oberton, Mrs A. Allen, Mr K.P. Blakemore, Mrs Phyllis Bushill-Matthews, Mrs Donald Harvey, Mrs Joyce Davies and Mrs Payne Paget.

Thanks are also due to a number of archivists who supplied information on the botanical gardens of their areas.

I owe my thanks to Angela Oldfield for typing the manuscript, to Dave Roach, Ron Swift and Geoff Dowling, who undertook much of the photographic reproduction work, to Jean Dowling and Carl Burness who re-drew three of the Garden plans and to Genevieve Andrews for the general index.

Last, but not least, my husband and my mother gave me much encouragement and support.   P.B.

The Birmingham Botanical and Horticultural Society gratefully acknowledges the financial help towards the publication of this book provided by the following organisations and individuals:

The Birmingham Common Good Fund; The Feeney Trust; The Friends of the Birmingham Botanical Gardens; The Hugh and Anne Kenrick Trust; The Royal Horticultural Society; The Stanley Smith Horticultural Trust; Miss D.A. Cadbury; Professor and Mrs J.G. Hawkes; Dr and Mrs R.N. Lester; Mr P.G. Lloyd; Mr and Mrs Stephen Lloyd; Mrs H.H. Taylor.

The author and publishers wish to thank the following people and institutions for kindly supplying illustrations and giving permission for their reproduction in this book: Mrs A. Allen for the illustration on p. 89; the Archive Film Agency: pp. 92, 93; the Birmingham Botanical and Horticultural Society: pp. 25, 43, 47, 61, 63, 71, 72, 73 (bottom), 75, 76, 87, 88 (top), 90, (top and bottom), 102-3, and plates 10, 11 and 13; Birmingham Museum and Art Gallery: p. 29; Birmingham Reference Library: pp. 48, 49 (bottom), 79, 100, 101, and plate 6; the Council of the Linnean Society of London: p. 17; Hugh and Anne Kenrick: plate 8; Paul Morby: p. 105.

'In the Birmingham Botanic Gardens one feels
in the country, far away from the din of
commerce, the roar of trade, and the contentions
of politics.'
Gardeners' Chronicle, 28 September 1872

These words, written in 1872 – forty years after the gardens were
opened – remain true today, and this book is dedicated to those
who created and have since maintained such an oasis of delight.

Introduction

This book has been written to mark the celebration of one hundred and fifty years since the opening of the Birmingham Botanical and Horticultural Society's Gardens in Edgbaston on 11 June 1832. Although the founding of the Gardens was in line with similar developments in other centres of expanding urban population in the nineteenth century, the Gardens of the BBHS are unique in that they are the only provincial botanical gardens from that period that are still owned and administered by a private society. However, a history is justified beyond the claims of mere survival, for they have had a role of considerable significance in the lives of successive generations of the inhabitants of the West Midlands and continue to hold a special place in their affections. This book records the achievements as well as the vicissitudes of the Gardens' one hundred and fifty years.

The first fifty years of the nineteenth century saw the founding of about seventeen botanic gardens in Britain, in contrast to the six botanic gardens established from the seventeenth century onwards, beginning with Oxford (1621) and followed by Edinburgh (1670), the Chelsea Physic Garden (1673), Glasgow (1705), Cambridge (1760), and Glasnevin (1796). Apart from the Chelsea Physic Garden, founded by the Worshipful Society of Apothecaries, and the gardens of the Dublin Society at Glasnevin, these botanic gardens were adjuncts of the universities and provided living material for the study of botany relevant to the training of physicians. The early botanic gardens in England had been inspired by the gardens associated with the universities of northern Italy, beginning with Pisa in 1543, and subsequently emulated by the major universities of northern Europe.

In addition to the institutional botanic gardens, certain private individuals also laid out botanic gardens, of which the most famous in England was the Royal Garden at Kew established by Princess Augusta in 1753.

The botanic gardens founded in Britain in the nineteenth century differed in several important respects from their predecessors. The majority were not associated with the universities,[1] but were founded by private botanical and horticultural societies with a membership of amateur botanists and horticulturalists. These societies were self-financing and only exceptionally received grants from national or university funds.[2] Their aims were to promote the study of botany and the practice of horticulture among middle-class subscribers who were engaged in the professions, commerce or industry. For such men, botany and horticulture were recreational activities of considerable importance. The botanical gardens of private societies also had a secondary purpose. They were landscaped to include ornamental features in addition to the botanical collections, and they thereby provided a place of amenity of a semi-private character.

The impetus for the formation of botanic

gardens in the nineteenth century came from the host of plant introductions which were flooding into Britain from the far corners of the globe. John Claudius Loudon estimated that, by the end of the eighteenth century, of the 13,140 species in cultivation in Britain only 1,400 were native. Approximately 5,000 of these introductions had come in the third quarter of the eighteenth century.[3] In the nineteenth century there was a startling increase, amounting to over 11,000 species.[4] These introductions comprised not only a wide range of herbaceous species, shrubs and trees, particularly conifers suitable for outdoor cultivation, but also a large number of exotics, among which orchids were highly prized. It was obviously beyond the resources of any one individual to acquire all these species; but, by common action in the promotion of a botanical garden, access was afforded to a representative collection of old and new introductions. Private individuals could also augment their own collections at minimal cost by participating in a system of exchange with such institutions.

Clearly there was a certain degree of emulation in the establishment of botanic gardens in the first half of the nineteenth century, and the example set by the Liverpool Gardens which opened in 1802, largely through the influence of William Roscoe, led to similar gardens at Hull (1812), Glasgow (1817), the London Horticultural Society's Gardens in Kensington (1818) which were moved to Chiswick in 1821, the Caledonian Society's Gardens in Edinburgh (1820), Manchester (1829), Belfast (1829), Birmingham (1832), Bath (1834), Sheffield (1836), Leeds (1840) and the Royal Botanic Society of London Gardens in Regent's Park (1841). Botanic gardens were also established at Wakefield and Bury St. Edmunds, and some societies promoted joint zoological and botanical gardens, such as Bristol, Cheltenham and the Royal Surrey Zoological Gardens near Camberwell, all opened in the 1830s.

Although this book necessarily concen-

trates on the history of one botanic garden, the Garden of the Birmingham Botanical and Horticultural Society had several points of similarity with the others founded in the nineteenth century. Like them it was opened in order to encourage the study of botany and foster horticultural skills among the middle-class shareholders who subscribed the capital. Initially there was much enthusiasm, and a high standard of excellence was achieved, though it was soon apparent that the level of financial support fell short of what was required for its continuing maintenance. Over the years the BBHS, in common with other societies, had to resort to the introduction of more popular features to widen the basis of support, and the botanical and horticultural aspects at times assumed a secondary significance. But although there have been few periods when the Society was entirely free of financial preoccupations, a policy of cautious and dedicated management has ensured that it escaped the fate of the other provincial societies whose greater financial problems caused their disbandment and, in some cases, closure.

One additional factor has been of considerable significance in the continuing viability of the Birmingham Gardens, and has arisen from the choice of a site on the Edgbaston estate of the Calthorpe family. The estate has been in the ownership of the family since 1717, and from 1786 onwards building leases were granted on it. A policy of residential development was strictly enforced by covenants, and the estate attracted many Birmingham merchants, manufacturers and professional men. In addition, a limited number of leases were granted to institutions, and when the Society approached Lord Calthorpe's agent, Mr Harris, with a view to acquiring a site in Edgbaston, he advised the granting of a lease on the grounds that it would 'greatly promote the interest of the estate'.[5]

The Gardens were sited in the central area of the estate, which was characterised by detached villas set in sizeable grounds. Recognising that the Gardens formed an important amenity in this area of the estate, and would be an additional inducement to those considering applying for building leases for villas, the Calthorpes supported them by charging a low annual ground rent and offering sizeable contributions to successive appeals for funds. Although, in the opinion of one writer, without the support of the Calthorpes 'the Society would certainly have collapsed',[6] due recognition must also be given to many other individuals, not all of them Edgbaston residents, who served on the committees in a voluntary capacity, and who also responded generously to appeals for funds. If, likewise, their motives were not wholly altruistic, for the Gardens provided them with a centre of botanical and horticultural knowledge within a spectacular setting, these facilities were also made available to a wide section of society, which has long enjoyed 'the oasis of delight' that is provided by the Gardens of the Birmingham Botanical and Horticultural Society.

Botanical Names

Apart from a few spelling corrections the botanical names mentioned in the text are taken verbatim from the original sources. Since many of these names are no longer correct the current synonyms are given in the index.

1

A Promising Beginning
1829-1845

In 1829 when the proposal to establish a botanic garden in the neighbourhood of Birmingham was launched, four other towns – Liverpool, Hull, Glasgow and Manchester – had already successfully established similar gardens. The scheme proposed was in fact the second such project that had been considered in Birmingham. In 1801 subscriptions had been invited for the formation of a botanic garden of two acres. The idea had probably originated with James Clarke, a druggist, who had been elected treasurer of a society formed to adopt a code of laws and collect subscriptions. Although the society had attracted the support of Matthew Boulton, one of the town's leading manufacturers, who chaired a meeting of subscribers held on 10 November 1801, the number of subscribers had apparently been insufficent, and the project lapsed. The failure of this first scheme was, in part, a reflection of the social and economic character of Birmingham itself. Although some merchants and manufacturers, including Matthew Boulton himself, had derived substantial wealth from Birmingham's staple trades of guns, toys and brass, they were few in number. Trade in Birmingham, with the exception of guns, was generally depressed, owing to the loss of European markets as a result of the Napoleonic wars.

Twenty-eight years later the industries of Birmingham were in a more flourishing state. The population of the town had grown from 60,822 in 1801 to 110,914 in 1831. Residence in the town had become increasingly unattractive as formerly exclusive residential areas succumbed to commercial and industrial development, and many of the well-to-do had emulated the pattern established by their predecessors of seeking residence in the rural hinterland of Birmingham at a distance from the smoke, grime and noise of the town from which their wealth was derived. For them a botanic garden would fulfil various needs. Here they could study the accelerating number of species being introduced into Britain, as well as learn how to cultivate them and observe which species would flourish in their own gardens. Those who already possessed sizeable collections of plants themselves could augment them by exchange, donating duplicates to the botanic garden and acquiring new species in return. For others of the middle class whose occupations dictated continued residence in the town, a botanic garden would not only provide a place for scientific study but also a semi-private garden for recreation.

On 9 July 1829 the High Bailiff, Thomas Lee, chaired a meeting held in the Old Library which passed the following resolutions:

That it is desirable to form a Botanical and Horticultural Society in the neighbourhood of Birmingham.

That, for this purpose, Four hundred Shares be raised, at £5 per share, and that each share be subjected to a subscription of one guinea per annum.

The promoters of the scheme recognised that their efforts would be attended with greater success if they could enlist the patronage of the local nobility, and the Earl of Dartmouth was approached for his support. He agreed to take the chair at a meeting of shareholders held at the Royal Hotel on 3 September 1829, and was elected President. A code of laws was discussed and a committee of management elected who were to 'fix a site for the gardens, and to carry the objects of the Society into effect'. The meeting closed on an optimistic note:

> A very warm and general feeling prevails in favour of the undertaking, and there is no doubt but that it will be attended by success.[1]

Further names were added to the list of patrons, including the Duke of Sussex and several of the principal landowners in the area, such as Earl Howe, Earl Mountnorris, Lord Lyttelton, Lord Calthorpe, Sir Edward Dolman Scott and Chandos Leigh. William Withering, whose father had been a physician to the General Hospital and was renowned for his introduction of digitalis in the treatment of heart diseases, also acted as a patron.

The Committee itself, on whose abilities the success of the project largely depended, numbered twenty-four and included men who were already experienced in the management of charitable institutions and societies in the town. The originators of the scheme, James Armitage, a manufacturing chemist, and John Darwall, a physician, acted as Joint Honorary Treasurers, and Thomas Knott, the proprietor of *Aris's Gazette*, was the Honorary Secretary. The Committee also comprised four leading attorneys, James Beswick, George Barker, J.W. Whateley and John Meredith; two Anglican clergymen, the Rev. George Peake, and Rev. James Pearson; two bankers, Isaac Spooner and Timothy Smith; three physicians, J.W. Crompton, Edward

Johnstone and John Johnstone; two merchants, George Hadley and W.H. Osborn; and six manufacturers, Henry Hunt, J.T. Lawrence, Francis Lloyd, J.F. Ledsam, John Linwood, Edward Thomason and Joseph Walker. James Taylor, a banker, and Thomas Lee, a merchant, acted as Trustees.

In April 1830 the Committee began the task of acquiring suitable land for the establishment of the Gardens and advertised for a site which they stipulated should not be in excess of twenty acres and should be situated within three miles of the centre of the town. There was an immediate response from the owners or leaseholders of four sites, and an experienced gardener, William Lunn, was retained to accompany the Committee to inspect these sites. Dr Darwall reported their findings to a general meeting of shareholders on 19 October.[2]

Lunn favoured the establishment of the Gardens on a portion of the grounds of the Aston Hall estate, which was owned at that time by the Warwick bankers, Messrs Greenway and Greaves. However, the tenant of Aston Hall, James Watt, the younger, had viewed these proposals with alarm, and Dr Darwall had to report that 'from the unwillingness ... of the present occupier of Aston Hall to have a garden in his neighbourhood, the proprietors of the Estate decline letting it for that purpose'.

A site in Edgbaston used as a strawberry garden also proved unsuitable, as the proposed rent was considered too high. The offer by Theodore Price, a nailmaster, of land on his Harborne Park estate was rejected because, although the land had advantages of access, it was found to have cold soil. The fourth site appeared to be the most advantageous. John Aspley, a fire insurance agent, had a twenty-five years' lease from Lord Calthorpe, of sixteen acres at Edgbaston, situated on Westbourne Road, two miles from the centre of the town. Aspley had proposed that the Society take over his lease on twelve acres of the land, which was used as pasture for a small hobby farm.

Of this land Lunn had reported:

> I find it contains a mixture of soil, suitable for Botanical and Horticultural purposes – good loam bog and clay for bricks – a small brook with detached springs on the ground, considered of a permanent nature – the site commands a bold southern aspect, well protected from the north-east and north-west winds; has a pleasing view of Edgbaston Park, and an extensive view of the surrounding country. I should also observe, that the land on the east side of Holly Bank, is occupied by Mr William Phipson of Westbourne, which grounds join the Worcester Canal.

The Committee then approached Lord Calthorpe's agent, Mr Harris, who arranged to lease the land to the Society at an annual rent of £100. The Committee soon saw that it would be desirable to acquire all the land leased by Aspley, and to include his villa, Holly Bank, its pleasure grounds, kitchen garden and remaining pasture land in the botanic garden, as these occupied the apex of the site.

When Aspley was consulted he replied that 'he would prefer not being disturbed', but that if the Society considered the land of importance he would let it to them for the remainder of the lease. The Society then entered into lengthy negotiations with Aspley, which were not concluded until June 1831, when the Society finally agreed on a price for buying the lease rather than renting the additional four acres.

Having secured an option on the twelve-acre site, the Committee had turned their attention to the appointment of a Curator, though they recognised that it was unlikely that the Society would be 'fortunate enough to meet with a thorough landscape gardener and a practical cultivator in the same person'.[3] An advertisement for a Curator was placed in December 1830, the appointment to carry a salary of £100 p.a. and a rent-free house and coals. There were five applicants. The Committee appointed Alexander Reith, who after accepting the post withdrew; and in February 1831 the

John Claudius Loudon, 1783-1843, who designed the layout of the Birmingham Botanical Gardens in 1831. Oil painting by J. Linnell, 1840-1.

post was offered to their second choice, David Cameron, who was then employed as head gardener to the banker Robert Barclay at Bury Hill near Dorking. His application was accompanied by six testimonials, including ones from John Claudius Loudon, Charles Loddiges and Charles Barclay, who had recently inherited Bury Hill from his father. Loudon's testimonial was couched in terms of the highest praise and emphasised Cameron's qualities as a practical cultivator:

> I never heard any gentleman say more in favour of his gardener than Mr Barclay did to me in favour of Mr Cameron, and I never saw a garden in higher order of keeping, or the plants in houses or in the open air in a more thriving state than at Bury Hill.[4]

Cameron, on his appointment, had indicated to the Committee that he had no skills as a landscape gardener,[5] and it was doubtless on his suggestion that Mr Ledsam and Mr Knott then approached

John Claudius Loudon about laying out the gardens. Loudon's response was immediate. He agreed to travel to Birmingham in May 1831 and to furnish a plan.

For the Committee this was satisfactory in more ways than one. Loudon was one of the most prominent landscape gardeners of the age, the proprietor of an influential periodical, *The Gardener's Magazine*, and the author of numerous works on botany and horticulture. He agreed to carry out the design solely on payment of his expenses for the journey and for residence while in Birmingham. A recent biographer of Loudon says that this shows his lack of business acumen, for carrying out the undertaking for such a small financial reward.[6] But such a view neglects Loudon's crusading zeal in the furtherance of his ideas and his willingness to promote the study of botany and horticulture among the middle classes.[7] Moreover in the preceding year he had married Jane Webb, the daughter of a Birmingham manufacturer, and a visit to Birmingham fitted in with the Loudons' plans for a tour of private gardens and commercial nurseries in the north of England. This could now begin with a pleasant interlude in Birmingham, enabling Jane Loudon to visit her Birmingham friends and Loudon to guide the fortunes of the infant project. Nor did Loudon neglect the opportunity to make an inspection of private gardens and commercial establishments in the vicinity of Birmingham, and these were subsequently reported on in *The Gardener's Magazine*.[8] Some of these establishments attracted high praise from Loudon, including George Barker's garden in Monument Lane, Edgbaston, James Taylor's grounds at Moor Green, the Handsworth nursery of John Pope and Sons and the metallic hothouse manufactory of John Jones and Co. in Mount Street, Birmingham.

Immediately after his arrival in Birmingham Loudon inspected the Holly Bank site and informed the Committee that it was 'absolutely necessary to the undertaking' that the gardens should include John Aspley's villa and pleasure ground, and the Committee agreed that his design should be for the entire sixteen-acre site.[9]

The Committee and Loudon were clearly in accord about the features to be incorporated in the layout of the Gardens, and members of the Committee had already been active in seeking the advice of those associated with similar establishments. A letter from Rees Davies, the Secretary of the Hull Botanic Gardens, dated 26 June 1829, indicated the problems of maintaining the botanic character of such gardens:

> When the Garden was projected it was intended to be more purely *botanical* than it is at present and this might arise from the circumstance of Mr Spencer, the entomologist, and Sir Peter Walton, botanist and author of *Dendrologia Brit.* being upon the Committee. As however they did not remain very long upon it, it was soon discovered that 99 out of 100 subscribers paid more attention to the pretty flowering plants in the stove and green house than to the botanical quarter which those gentlemen had laid out and which has been until recently very much neglected.[10]

John Shepherd, the Curator of the Liverpool Botanic Garden, writing in January 1831, cautioned the Committee against excessive ambition:

> Gentlemen are too apt to be carried away with the idea, of having one which will embrace everything connected with the profession and adopt a plan, which however theoretically correct will in the end be found to be very inconvenient ... my fears are that the union of horticultural and botanical departments will end in disappointment to the promoters of it.[11]

However, though the Committee were clearly aware of these considerations, their plans matched Loudon's own ideas. Loudon thoroughly approved of their intentions 'to combine a scientific with an ornamental garden, and these to a certain extent with a nursery and market garden so as by selling superfluous plants, fruits and culinary vegetables to lessen the annual

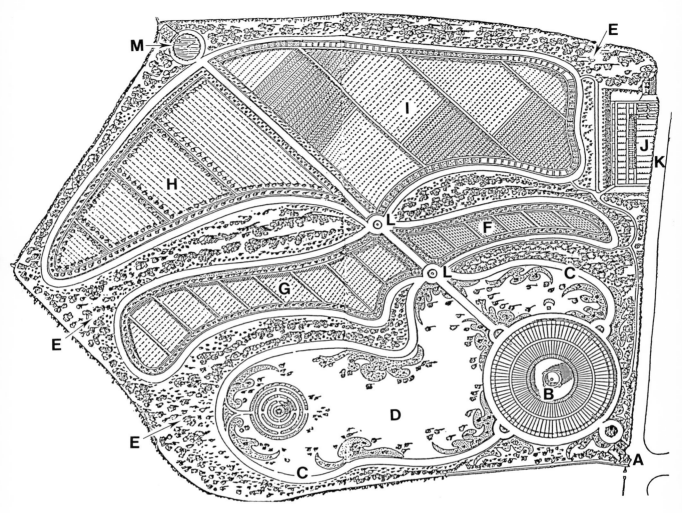

J.C. Loudon's plan of the layout of the Birmingham Botanical and Horticultural Society's Gardens, showing its expected appearance after 'several years' growth'. From *The Gardener's Magazine*, August 1832.

expenses of keeping'. Financial considerations also dictated that the plan should be capable of being executed by degrees 'as the finances of the Society allowed'. Loudon therefore executed a design that was a judicious mixture of the scientific and the ornamental, and one that utilised fully the advantages of the existing topography and the spectacular setting.[12]

Loudon's plan, as published in *The Gardener's Magazine* of August 1832, showed what the garden would look like after several years' growth. The main entrance (A) was sited at the junction of Vicarage and Westbourne Roads and included a lodge for the gatekeeper. It led immediately to a circular arrangement of glasshouses (B), positioned on the only available level ground at the apex of the site. This form was adopted to avoid an initial view of back sheds and walls which Loudon had been critical of at the Liverpool Botanic Gardens. From the main circular walk led a series of zig-zag gravelled paths intersecting the gardens (C), this being the most suitable way to

19

'descend with ease from the high to low grounds, and in like manner to ascend from the latter to the former', as there was a fall of sixty feet from the head to the bottom of the site. Within the confines of these paths were to be included the following: an area of pleasure grounds comprising a main lawn sited on a natural bowl with ornamental parterres for annuals, and a rosary comprising two and a half acres (D); botanical areas of trees, shrubs and perennials to be laid out on the Linnaean system in various parts of the gardens and occupying seven acres (E); a flower garden of a quarter of an acre (F); an American ground of three-quarters of an acre (G); an orchard and fruit nursery of one and a half acres (H); a kitchen garden and agricultural garden of two acres (I); and a reserve garden and experimental ground of an acre (J), with a wall heated by flues for peaches and nectarines (K) which would also act as a boundary wall. Additional features were a series of fountains at the main intersections of the walks (L) culminating in a 'grand jet' at the lowest point of the gardens (M), and the provision of grass walks in the botanical areas 'for those who prefer walking on turf', achieved by the spacing of the specimens. Aviaries and structures to accommodate animals could be placed in the pleasure grounds if the Society decided to add a zoological collection.

Loudon prepared two alternative designs for the glasshouses, both on a circular plan. His first design was for a circular double ring of hothouses with a central area including an ornamental tower to contain the steam-heating apparatus, a potting shed and water cisterns, which would be reached by an underground tunnel. In the first instance the outer portion of the circular houses overlooking the gardens would be erected and the sites for future houses would be temporarily laid out with borders for seedlings and rare plants. Meanwhile the existing villa would be retained as a house for the Curator and for the use of the Committee, and the heating apparatus would be installed and the connecting tunnel built. Loudon's second plan was for a spectacular conical structure 200 feet in diameter with a central height of 100 feet which could be erected 'if expense were not an object'. The interior area comprising an acre would be laid out in concentric beds and walks and be divided into four compartments for plants from different climatic zones, and these could be viewed from a circular winding walkway in the centre.

On 30 May 1831 Loudon attended a meeting of the Gardens Sub-Committee which noted that he had 'finished the outline of his plans for laying out the whole of the land and afterwards entered into a general explanation of it to the Committee'.[13] He then departed to continue his tour, confident that his plan had been well received and would be carried out in accordance with his instructions. Almost immediately, however, an ominous note was struck at the next meeting of the Gardens Sub-Committee on 2 June:

> The circular arrangements of the Conservatory and hot and green houses recommended by Mr Loudon, were, however, deemed by the Committee to be formed upon too expensive a scale and it was determined to invite designs and estimates of a less costly nature.

At this date there were several firms in Birmingham specialising in the design and manufacture of metallic hothouses, and the contract was awarded to Messrs John Jones and Company of Mount Street, Birmingham, a firm that had been in operation since 1818.[14] Their design was for a linear arrangement incorporating an elliptical conservatory flanked by stove houses with sloping roofs, to be erected at a cost of £1,660. The heating arrangements were by means of a steam boiler ordered from Benjamin Fowler of London, whose apparatus Loudon had recommended to Cameron.

Whether it was Cameron who eventually informed Loudon of the rejection of his plan for a circular range is not recorded, but there can be little doubt that he reacted with extreme displeasure:

> We found that a straight range of hothouses had been determined on; and a plan and elevation of this range have been subsequently shown to us. We entirely disapprove of it, and its position in the gardens; and we have no hesitation whatever in saying that we consider our design completely spoiled, as the general effect depended entirely on the glasshouses being circular in plan. We only regret that the committee have adopted our circuitous line of main walk (which, indeed, we staked out when on the spot), because we dislike exceedingly the idea of having our name associated in any degree, however slight, with a garden which, though it might have been one of the most perfect in its kind existing anywhere, and although unique in some arrangements, is now bungled, and never likely to reflect credit on any one connected with it.[15]

There is no recorded evidence that Loudon's disapproval registered with the Committee, and the work of laying out the gardens proceeded during 1831. With the exception of the arrangement of the glass-houses it was substantially in accordance with Loudon's plan.[16] The committee noted at their meeting of 25 October 1831 that 'the work of laying out the ground according to the plan recommended by Mr Loudon, with such alterations as the Committee under the advice of their curator have been induced to make, is proceeding as rapidly and satisfactorily as they could desire'. Cameron's alterations were of a minor character and consisted of the substitution of a straight terrace instead of a circular walk in front of the Conservatory and the inclusion of an area for aquatic plants formed by the enlargement of an existing pond on the site.

The first task had been to strengthen the existing boundaries of the site, and seedling hollies were planted along the line of hawthorn hedges, as recommended by Loudon. The hollies were obtained free of charge from the Wardens of Sutton Coldfield Park in August 1831. In the same month Messrs Rickman and Hutchinson, a local firm of architects, were awarded the contract to design the lodge entrance, and estimates were obtained for the fruit and boundary walls, and for gravelling the walks. Cameron's report on the progress made in laying out the grounds was read at the Annual General Meeting of shareholders on 9 July 1832. He reported:

> 1400 yards in length of the walks being gravelled, the arboretum being brought into form and planted with 1555 species and varieties of shrubs according to the natural system as soil and situation would permit, the American ground planted with one plant of a sort which are also included in the above number of species and varieties, the herbaceous ground has been planted in part with plants according to the Linnaean arrangement, the ground intended for fruit and vegetables has in part been trenched and is now nearly all under a crop of potatoes. The boundary wall is planted with peach, nectarine, apricot, cherry and plum trees, stocks for grafting and budding crab, pear, quince, plums and cherries are planted in the experimental ground ... The grass plat has by repeated mowing been brought to a tolerable good swarth.

The Gardens had been opened to shareholders in the previous month on Monday 11 June 1832, and could be visited daily from 8 a.m. to dusk. Shareholders, who were subject to an annual subscription of one guinea, had the right of free admission for themselves and members of their immediate family and up to four other persons. The fact that the Gardens were to be open on Sunday caused immediate protests from a group of Edgbaston residents, and though the Society did not accede to their request that they should be closed altogether on that day, from August onwards Sunday openings were to be from 3 p.m. to sunset and the hothouses were to be shut.

Loudon had envisaged that 'the planting of the botanic and ornamental gardens will amount to a very trifling expense; and it is supposed that almost all the plants will be received in presents, or in exchange, from other public establishments'.[17] This in fact was partly the case, though when the Gardens began to be laid out, Cameron placed an order to the value of £200 with

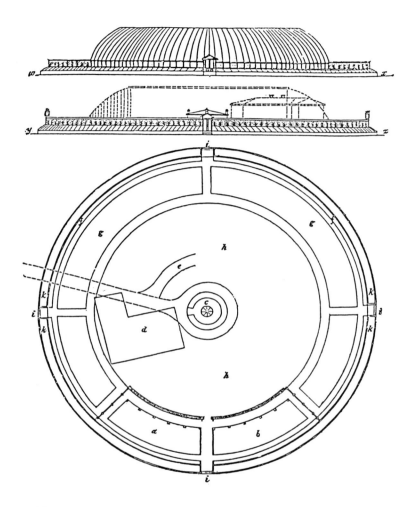

a, The conservatory.   b, The hot-house.
c, Steam apparatus, with the under-ground roadway round it.
d, House for the curator and council-room.   e, Inclined plane to the tunnel.
f, Border for trees to be trained on both sides of the fence, as shown in the north elevation.
g, Border for seedlings and rare plants, &c.
h h, Situation for hot-beds, and beds for seedlings; for rare or tender plants; and for setting
out the green-house plants, &c. &c.
, i i, &c., The four main entrances across the outside pits from the circular terrace.
k, The pits in four divisions, as in fig. 76.
w x, South elevation.   y z, North elevation.

J.C. Loudon's design for a circular range of glasshouses for the Birmingham Botanical
Gardens, 1831. *Left*: Plan and elevation of the initial layout to include a conservatory (a) and
hot-house (b) and a temporary arrangement of the area. *Right*: The full range. From *The
Gardener's Magazine*, August 1832.

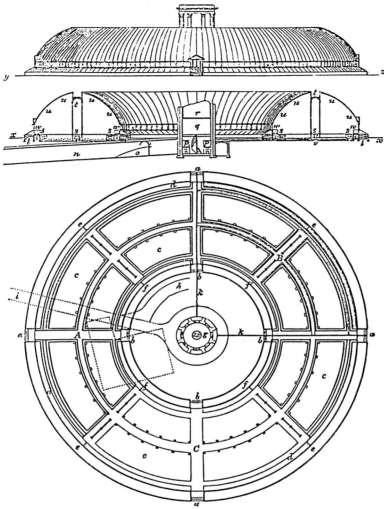

a a a a, The main entrances from the surrounding terrace.
b b b b, Corresponding entrances from the interior area.
c c c c, &c., Beds for large specimens to grow in the free soil.
d d, &c., Shelves for plants in pots.
e e e e, The exterior pit, in four divisions.
f f f f, The interior pit, in four divisions.
g, Central tower, in which is contained the steam or hot-water apparatus, in the cellar story, a potting-shed on the ground floor, and in the upper part a supply cistern for the hot-houses and jets. Round the base there is a vaulted passage, by which carts may pass round, unless it is considered preferable to ascend the inclined plane *h*, and drop the coals, through man-holes on the surface, to the cellars below.
h, Inclined plane to the tunnel.
i, Tunnel, which communicates with the base of the tower, the interior area, and the public road.
k, Mains of the steam or hot-water apparatus.

l l, Exterior pits.   *m m*, Interior pits.   *n*, Tunnel.
o, Archway, forming the entrance to the inclined plane which leads from the tunnel to the surface of the central area.
p p, Two steam or hot-water apparatus : either of these will supply heat to the whole range ; but two are recommended, in case of accident.
q, Potting-shed.   *r*, Cistern.
s s, Walks within the hot-houses.
t, Walk over them, in which, during winter, rolls of matting may be kept, for letting down over the glass to exclude the frost.
u u u u, Situation of pipes pierced with numerous small holes, for watering all the hot-houses, in imitation of a shower of rain, as at Messrs. Loddiges's.
v, Steam-pipes shown under the pathways.
w w w w, Benches for pots.
x x, Surface of the terrace walk.
y z, Elevation, taken opposite the centre of either of the four entrances.

23

Conrad Loddiges and Sons of London for 1300 trees and shrubs, including varieties of American plants. A number of fruit trees were also ordered from Donald Lowe and seeds were purchased from Hunnimans of London. In subsequent years these three firms sent many donations of plants and seeds to the Birmingham gardens. In August 1831 the Society received the first of many donations from the London Horticultural Society's Gardens at Chiswick. The gift comprised seventy-five species of plants, eleven types of ornamental seeds and forty crocus 'roots'.[18] Other gifts were received from the Liverpool Botanic Garden, which sent a consignment of 1000 herbaceous and other plants, and the Chelsea Physic Garden, which donated 152 plants. Private collectors were also generous. They included Charles Barclay of Bury Hill, Earl Mountnorris, who donated 400 plants and 19 palms and Crinums from his famous collection at Arley, Benjamin Maund of Bromsgrove, who gave 147 plants, and Mr Borrer, who donated 218. The list of donations from Birmingham men closely associated with the project was headed by James Armitage, who gave 114 plants; and others sent smaller quantities 'according to the extent of their collections', plants being received from William Withering and Messrs Linwood, Osborne, Crompton, Hadley, Bourne and Smallwood. Two commercial firms – Messrs Netland of Dorking and Messrs Pope and Sons of Handsworth – also donated plants.

In the following year donations continued to flood in, and by August 1832 it was estimated that the collection numbered between four and five thousand species. By 1833 this figure had risen to seven thousand. Many new species had been donated by the Botanic Gardens of Edinburgh, Glasgow, Oxford, Liverpool and Manchester, Cameron having visited these Gardens to collect seeds and select plants. Plants were also received from the Botanic Garden at Dublin, and the East India Company sent 'sixteen large plants

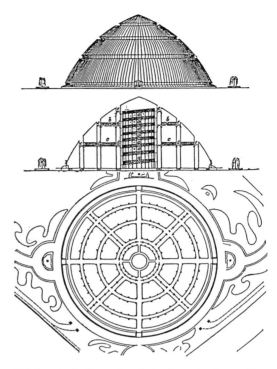

J.C. Loudon's alternative design for a glasshouse 'if expense were not an object'. The conical glasshouse would have a diameter of 200 ft and a central height of 100 ft. From *The Gardener's Magazine*, August 1832.

in a case' from their Botanic Gardens at Calcutta. John Williams, who was renowned for the breeding of new fruit varieties, sent several strawberry plants from his garden at Pitmaston in Worcester. Altogether in 1833 42 donors sent over 2,400 plants, and ten donors sent over 1300 seeds. These included 40 types of seeds from Australia donated by John Claudius Loudon, whose publicly vented anger must have cooled somewhat.[19]

By 1834 the Society had a collection of over 9,000 species, and at this date it was evidently among the best-stocked botanic gardens in Britain. It had assembled its collection with a speed comparable to that of the Glasgow Botanic Gardens, which four years after its foundation in 1817 had a

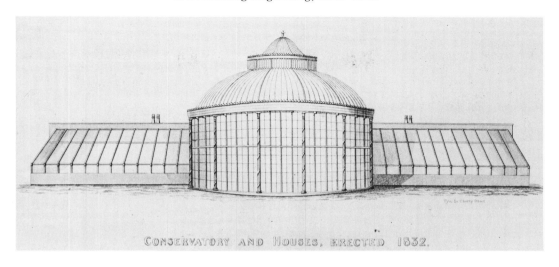

Conservatory and Hot-houses erected at the Birmingham Botanical Gardens in 1832, designed and executed by John Jones and Company, Mount Street, Birmingham.

collection of 9,000 species, of which 3,000 had been donated by Thomas Hopkirk.[20] The Birmingham collection in 1834 was probably more extensive than that of the London Horticultural Society's Gardens at Chiswick, opened in 1823, which numbered 10,000 species in 1840.[21]

In 1833 Cameron began despatching duplicates in the Society's collections to the botanic institutions, private collectors and commercial firms who had been the major donors of the collection and despatched to them over 1,000 plants.[22] Indeed this was the understanding behind the donation of plants. It was essentially a system of exchange which fostered the building up of collections at minimum cost. A noted private collector of the period, Robert Bevan of Bury St. Edmunds, put the position succinctly in a letter to Cameron in December 1841:

> I have received a lot of seeds and bulbs from Chile, of which I shall be happy to impart some to you, if agreeable. I am sure I can trust you to be liberal to me in return.

The Birmingham collection was not only extensive: it also included a large number of species recently introduced into cultivation, as can be judged from a letter received in 1841 from Sir William Hooker, shortly after he took up his appointment as Director of the Royal Botanic Gardens at Kew. Cameron had sent a number of plants for Kew and for Sir William Hooker's private garden of West Park:[23]

> Pray let me thank you in my own and Lady Hooker's name for the very nice plants you have been so good as to send me for my garden. They are just the kind of things I wished for and I hope when you come to see our Botanic Garden and select some things for yourself you will come on $\frac{3}{4}$ of a mile from there and look at the ground that you have thus helped to ornament.
>
> You have sent Smith some capital things. He declared that you had more that was new to us than any collection he visited in the north.

The Birmingham Botanic Gardens were especially noteworthy for their collection of Alpines and herbaceous plants, and two Societies in particular requested plants of this type. In January 1841 Dr Lindley, the Secretary of the London Horticultural Society, wrote to Cameron requesting a collection of Alpines for the rockwork in front of the Conservatory. Cameron despatched a parcel of 170 Alpine plants.[24] In the same year Cameron sent the Royal

Botanic Society of London 208 species of herbaceous plants for the gardens which were being laid out in Regent's Park. Cameron had visited London in May 1841 to attend a LHS show and had visited several gardens and nurseries, including the Regent's Park Garden; and no doubt its Curator, Richard Marnock, had placed his request at that time.[25]

Cameron's contacts with botanic institutions were not restricted to Britain alone but extended to the Continent and further afield. In 1833 Cameron had received seeds from the Royal Botanic Gardens of Berlin, and several exchanges of material were made in ensuing years. Plants and seeds were also received from the Botanic Gardens of Hamburg, Vienna, Naples and St. Petersburg, as well as from Sydney and Calcutta.

Important as these contacts were in building up the collections in the early years, one other factor had been of considerable significance. Among the Committee members and shareholders of the Society were a number of men who had a pronounced interest in horticulture, particularly in growing exotics. They also participated in the network of exchange of plants and were generous in their donations to the Society. Some of these men were in business as foreign merchants and instructed their agents to collect seeds and plants. Prominent among them were Charles Shaw, J.W. Crompton, E.W. Fry and Henry Van Wart, and many American species were added to the collections on their initiative. Others were professional men or manufacturers, of whom the most prominent was the attorney, George Barker, who financed his own collection in Mexico. Howard Luckcock, a jewellery manufacturer, also had extensive contacts with private collectors, as did John Willmore, a Birmingham manufacturer. Willmore was also renowned for his work in the creation of new varieties of heathers and other plants by hybridisation, and he supplied the Gardens with much interesting material.

It was not only the major donors of plants and seeds, however, who were included in the system of distribution operating in the early years of the Gardens: those who had contributed financially by taking out shares in the Society were also supplied with material. This began in 1834 when it was announced that Cameron had prepared 320 packets of seeds for distribution to shareholders, which included flower seeds 'all showy and deserving a place in every garden' and a winter salad vegetable called 'Normandy Cup'. 'Its good quality and times of sowing may be seen at the Gardens.' Shareholders were also advised that they could apply for surplus dahlia roots and twenty plants each of various kinds of strawberries. In the following spring 189 varieties of apples, pears, plums and cherries would also be distributed.[26]

In the following year 4,500 packets of seeds were distributed to shareholders, and in 1839 Cameron prepared 10,000 packets of flower seeds for distribution. Although in most years the types of seeds were not named, a full list appeared in the annual report for 1841, and these included seeds of Californian poppy, evening primrose, delphinium, arabis, silene, mignonette and French honeysuckle.

So pronounced was the interest in the collection and cultivation of exotics in Birmingham in the 1830s that the joint secretaries of the Society together edited an illustrated botanical magazine, a venture rarely embarked upon by provincial botanical societies. G.B. Knowles, who was professor of botany at the Birmingham Royal School of Medicine, and Frederic Westcott, who also lectured in botany, had become joint honorary secretaries of the Society in 1833.

The Birmingham Botanic Garden or Midland Floral Magazine, subsequently renamed *The Floral Cabinet or Magazine of Exotic Botany*, appeared in monthly instalments from September 1836 and continued until December 1839. Its format was closely modelled on *Curtis's Botanical*

Magazine, and it contained 'accurate delineations, with botanical and popular descriptions of plants cultivated in the stove, the greenhouse or the open garden, and remarkable either for their beauty, their rarity, or the singularity of their structure'.

This periodical is a valuable source of evidence for the species in cultivation in the Gardens in their early years and also provides additional information on the means by which the plants reached Birmingham. As already noted, several species cultivated at Birmingham were new introductions, and Knowles and Westcott were responsible for the type descriptions of twenty species, though some were subsequently reclassified as synonyms.

Three new introductions were South American species acquired by the Society in 1835. *Malva concinna* and *Lathyrus purpureo-caeruleus* were donated by Charles Shaw and *Macrochilus fryanus* was the gift of E.W. Fry. This orchid was featured in one of the plates and included in the spectacular frontispiece to volume one. George Barker was responsible for the introduction of two Mexican species – *Solanum rossii* and *Begonia barkeri*, named by Knowles and Westcott in honour of their collector and his patron. Cameron's work is also commemorated in the naming of *Hibiscus cameronii*, which was added to the collection in 1837. The plant was raised from seeds donated by the Rev. John Angell James, the Minister of Carr's Lane Congregational Chapel, Birmingham, who had been sent the seeds by missionaries in Madagascar. Another rarity from Madagascar was *Tanghinia veneniflua*, the poison flowing Tanghin, used as an ordeal plant in its native land. This was raised from cuttings presented by Charles Barclay of Bury Hill, who had been sent seeds of the plant collected in Madagascar by Charles Telfair.

A number of local artists were responsible for the illustrations in *The Floral Cabinet*, including the daughter of the Curator, Frances Cameron. In 1838 she illustrated *Oxalis darvalliana* – 'named in compliment to Dr Darwall with whom and the late Mr Armitage the BBHS had its origin', and she also illustrated *Tradescantia spicata*, another new introduction by George Barker.

The Society also possessed a specimen of *Ceanothus collinus*, raised from seeds collected by one of the most famous of the early nineteenth-century collectors, David Douglas. His expedition to North America in 1826/7 had been sponsored by the London Horticultural Society, which had distributed seeds to various public and private establishments, including Messrs John Pope and Sons of Handsworth, who in turn donated them to the Society. The specimen at the Gardens was claimed to be 'the only one in the kingdom'. Another rarity. *Pentstemon mackayanus*, had been collected by Thomas Drummond in Mexico in 1834, and the seeds sent to Murray, the Curator of the Glasgow Botanic Garden, who then sent them to J.T. Mackay, the Curator of the Botanic Garden of Trinity College Dublin. Seeds of this plant were included among those sent to the BBHS from Dublin in 1836, and Knowles and Westcott noted that 'they had comfort in presenting it as the Dublin plant perished last winter'. Among the important accessions from European botanical gardens were specimens of *Rehmannia chinensis*, a native of North China. These were included in a large consignment of plants dispatched to the Gardens in the autumn of 1835 by Mr Otto, the Curator of the Royal Botanic Gardens at Berlin, 'to whom the Society are indebted for many rare and valuable additions to the collection'.

As well as descriptions and illustrations of plants, *The Floral Cabinet* included articles written by Cameron to foster horticultural knowledge. He wrote about the cultivation of orchids, camellias, dahlias and pelargoniums, as well as providing a monthly calendar of gardening operations. In 1837 Knowles and Westcott published an item of special relevance to Birmingham subscribers, written by Cameron. This was a list with comments on thirty-seven species 'not generally considered hardy' which had nevertheless been successfully grown out of doors at the Gardens. Two further articles by Cameron, concerning the effects of frost on the collections of trees and shrubs in the Gardens in the winters of 1837/8 and 1840/1, were published in *The Gardener's Magazine* and *The Gardeners' Chronicle* respectively.

Some other plants cultivated at the Gardens were illustrated in *The Botanist*, a similar periodical to *The Floral Cabinet*, edited by the Bromsgrove bookseller Benjamin Maund between 1837 and 1842. These included species of hibiscus, mimulus, dahlia and fuchsia. Varieties of ericas bred by John Willmore were also illustrated.

As well as supporting the publication of a botanical magazine, the Committee had wished to publish a complete catalogue of its collection. Unfortunately lack of funds prevented this project from being realised, apart from what was intended to be the first of eight parts, and a 'Catalogue of the Trees and Shrubs' prepared by Knowles and Westcott was published in 1836. This was arranged according to the de Candolle natural system with the equivalent Linnaean categories. In addition to the Latin name, the English name was given where appropriate, and also the date of introduction into the British Isles if known, the preferred soil, and a reference to an authoritative botanical work in which the species was figured. Synonyms were also mentioned in certain cases.

The list comprised 713 species and varieties, and is reproduced on pp. 121-38. Significantly, of the 354 species whose date of introduction was known over one third had been introduced between 1800 and 1833.

The collection included not only ornamental trees and shrubs but also fruit trees. Of the latter there were over 30 species of *Prunus*, including plums, cherries, almonds and bird cherries, 18 species of *Pyrus* (apples and pears) and about 30 species of *Rubus*, including blackberries, raspberries, etc.

Of the ornamental shrubs the collection was particularly rich in *Crataegus* or ornamental thorns, of which there were 56 species and varieties.[27] Some of these were recent introductions such as *Crataegus mexicana*, introduced from Mexico in 1827, *C. nigra* from Hungary in 1819 and *C. olivieriana* from Asia Minor in 1828. The extensive collection of roses comprised over 50 species of roses mainly introduced from India, China, Persia, N. America and Siberia in the late eighteenth and early nineteenth centuries. Interesting recent introductions were *Rosa microphylla* from the E. Indies in 1823 and *R. pygmaea* from the Caucasus in 1820. In addition there were 33 varieties of garden roses.

The collection also comprised 48 species and varieties of holly, several of which had been introduced from N. America. Likewise the collection of 16 species of magnolia included several N. American species, together with the hybrid *M. × soulangiana*, first cultivated in 1826 and still a popular garden variety. The collection of 18 species of clematis included several species still frequently in cultivation today, such as *C. flammula* introduced from S. Europe in 1597, *C. orientalis* from the Levant in 1731 and *C. macropetala* from Central Asia in 1827. Central Asian species were also represented in the collection of ten species of cotoneaster, of which six had been introduced from Nepal in the 1820s, such as *C. frigidus* and *C. microphyllus*, still in cultivation today.

Some of the more recent introductions, however, were from Europe, and the collection of 36 helianthemums or rock roses included *H. alpestre* introduced from Germany in 1818, and *H. barrelieri* from Italy in 1820. There were 16 species of *Cistus* in the collections, also introduced from Europe.

The collection of ornamental trees had a large group of acers (ornamental maples),

Pencil sketch of the Conservatory and Hot-houses, September 1839.

of which there were over 20 species, including the still popular *A. palmatum* introduced from Japan in 1820 and *A. macrophyllum* from N. America in 1826. There were also 9 species of *Aesculus* (horse chestnuts) including two recent introductions from N. America – *A. rubicunda* and *A. macrostachya* brought to Britain in 1820 and 1830 respectively.

At this point we must return to the progress of the Gardens in the years following their opening. Although Cameron continued to develop the Gardens in the manner envisaged by Loudon, he was forced to make one or two minor modifications. In 1834 he planted 250 laurels and 200 spruce 'for shelter in the arboretum and to make that position of the garden look more green in winter' – an action contrary to Loudon's explicit instructions that 'not a single plant be introduced for the

purposes of shelter or immediate effect', but necessitated by the force of the prevailing winds. For the same reason in 1835 a beech hedge was planted around the American ground, and in 1838 200 rhododendrons were added to the botanical area above the American ground. In the same year an orchid house was erected to accommodate the increasing numbers of specimens the Society possessed.

Among the distinguished visitors to the Gardens in 1839 was John Loudon, and he reported his impressions in the August issue of *The Gardener's Magazine*. Predictably, he described the Conservatory as 'one of the worst in point of taste that we know of', but he had nothing but praise for the management of the Gardens, which he attributed chiefly to the skill of David Cameron. The planting of the American ground drew high praise:

Such masses of the more rare dwarf rhododendrons and azaleas, vacciniums, kalmias, *Andromeda squarrosa* and *hypnoides*, *Cornus canadensis*, *Gaultheria shallon*, *Linnaea borealis* and similar plants, we have never seen elsewhere. We also observed *Amygdalus pumila* and other species of *Amygdalus*, *Prunus* and *Cerasus*, which compared with the same species in the smoky atmosphere of the London gardens, are like different species.

He was also impressed by the collection of alpine plants in pots 'a number of which are not to be found in any other garden', and the excellence of the herbaceous collection 'believed to be the most complete in Britain'. He concluded:

> On the whole, we were highly gratified with this garden, and especially with the growth of the trees and shrubs, as a consequence chiefly of the manner in which they have been managed, though partly also to the excellence of the situation. Mr Cameron has promised us the dimensions of some of the most rapid-growing kinds; and also drawings by his daughter, Miss Cameron, of some of the rare shrubs which we have never before seen in flower.

In 1844 *The Gardeners' Chronicle* published a lengthy report on the Birmingham Botanic Garden[28] which, though it attested to the flourishing condition of the collections, also hinted at the financial difficulties – a subject that will be discussed later:

> This garden still maintains its position, and although not supported with the liberality which might be expected from such a populous and wealthy neighbourhood, is nevertheless firmly established with a slightly-increasing income – a satisfactory circumstance which will be gratifying to those who feel an interest in everything that has a tendency to promote and extend this useful branch of natural history. Many of the shrubs and trees are beginning to develop their forms and specific characters; and these are times, and this too a locality, when such glorious objects, collected from all countries, and brought together by great enterprise and capital, will in the end be rightly appreciated and supported.

The writer found much to praise in the gardens, though he made some highly critical remarks on the positioning of the

hothouses, which he considered were 'exposed to the bleak and scourging winds that prevail in this district, and which gave them, even in summer, a cold and desolate hue when viewed in connection with the surrounding vegetation'.

The collection of ferns, which by this date numbered 360 species, was described as including many rarities. The pride of the collection was the Killarney fern, *Trichomanes brevisetum* var. *andrewsii*, which 'although a native of Ireland is not now to be found there'. *Phyllopodium rigidum* was thriving well, as were the rare winter greens, *Pyrola uniflora* and *P. secunda*. The collection of conifers was also highly praised, and Cameron was commended for his planting of certain species in high dry situations to avoid damage from late frosts. Particularly impressive were the recently introduced Mexican species, including *Pinus hartwegii*, *P. teocote*, *P. pseudostrobus* and *P. patula*:

> We may calculate upon seeing those magnificent trees from the high parts of Mexico, forming objects of as much interest as those from the north-west part of the same continent.

The writer considered that one of the most remarkable plants in the whole garden was *Fuchsia discolor*, which had attained a height of six feet and was covered in flowers and fruit. This had initially been planted in the greenhouse and had failed to flower but had thrived when planted out of doors:

> These judicious trials of exposing plants will do much to place a proper value on those from the high regions of tropical countries, and will read a lesson to many who select warm nooks and sheltered sites for plants otherwise accustomed to brave the scourge of the four winds of heaven.

The Society was active from its earliest years in promoting horticultural exhibitions, an important function that was also undertaken by similar societies. As early as 1829 William Withering, the younger, had written to the Society strongly recommending the holding of competitive exhibitions,[29] and in February 1830 John Sabine, the Secretary of the London Horticultural Society, had placed one of the Society's large silver medals at the disposal of the BBHS.[30]

The first exhibitions took place on 19 and 20 June 1833 at the Society of Arts rooms in New Street. This event was highly successful and was attended by numerous members of the Society and their families 'comprising most of the respectable residents of the town and its vicinity'. The exhibits numbered 'considerably above four hundred' and were 'pronounced by competent judges to be one of the finest collections of rare and choice plants ever brought together in this country'.[31]

The exhibits were organised in seven classes as follows:

> Class I The rarest plant in flower or the most recent introduction into Europe.
> Class II The most remarkable plant for its perfection in foliage, flower and general growth.
> Class III The largest number of fine specimens of plants.
> Class IV The finest specimens of forced fruit.
> Class V The finest specimens of fruit grown in the open garden.
> Class VI The earliest and finest specimen of forced vegetable.
> Class VII The finest specimen of vegetables grown in the open garden.[32]

These classes not only reflected the major areas of horticultural interest at the time, but also indicated that the aim was to attract entries from the wealthiest sections of society with the means to maintain hot-houses and employ knowledgeable gardeners. Further two-day exhibitions were held at the Gardens in July and August. Patrons, officers and shareholders were prominent among the prize-winners, and included the Earl of Dartmouth, Sir E.D. Scott, Lord Lyttelton, James Taylor, John Willmore, William Chance, W.H. Osborn, Thomas Clark, Mrs Taylor and John Linwood; and several prizes were awarded to Messrs John Pope and Sons of Handsworth. Other prize-winners included Earl Grey of Groby, Sir Charles

Throckmorton, Sir Rowland Hill and Harry Greswolde; and the Society acknowledged its indebtedness to members of the nobility and gentry, 'who have, at their own expense, forwarded the choicest productions of their gardens'.[33]

This initial success prompted the Society to embark on a considerable number of exhibitions in the following year, and monthly shows were promoted between March and November. John Willmore was awarded the London Horticultural Society's medal for 'having exhibited during the past year many fine hybrids of superior merit raised from seeds at Oldford, of 'Calceolarias, Ericas, *Petunia Willmoreana* and *Amaryllis Willmoreana*'.[34]

After two years of holding exhibitions the Society considered them to be highly successful in promoting horticultural skills:

> The Committee congratulate the Proprietors, and indeed the neighbourhood generally, on the fine displays of plants, fruits and culinary vegetables which they have produced; and on the spirit of emulation they have excited – a spirit which cannot fail to promote and extend the tastes for Botany and Horticulture and every branch of Floriculture.[35]

In the following year the number of exhibitions was reduced to four, but the expenses incurred in the arrangements and the provision of prizes resulted in a loss. In 1836 it was decided to promote exhibitions jointly with the Warwickshire Floral and Horticultural Society, 'to avoid too frequent recurrence of exhibitions'. This too was financially unsuccessful, and of the six shows held between April and September only the May show made a profit. In 1837 the Society returned to its original policy of promoting its own exhibitions which were held three times a year either at the Gardens or in the recently erected Town Hall, and musical interludes were provided by a military band or, in the Town Hall, by recitals on the organ.

Full lists of prize-winners were, as in

previous years, published in *Aris's Gazette*, and from 1841 also appeared in the national gardening periodical, *The Gardeners' Chronicle*, started in that year. The number of classes was considerably extended and included ferns, cacti, pelargoniums, florists' flowers, herbaceous plants and native orchids in addition to orchids, stove and glasshouse plants and fruit and vegetables. Special classes for cottagers and artisans were introduced in 1837, which in spite of the 2/6d entry fee attracted a considerable number of exhibits. The prize lists predominantly comprised the names of Birmingham and Black Country amateur horticulturalists, and only exceptionally included members of the aristocracy, such as the Earl of Dartmouth and the Earl of Stamford. The names of George Barker and John Willmore occurred with great regularity, and Birmingham manufacturers such as W.C. Alston and Josiah Mason were frequent prize-winners. The Annual Report for 1841 noted that George Barker and W.C. Alston had also gained awards at the London Horticultural Society's exhibitions.

Although the Society's aims were predominantly scientific, the Gardens were also the setting for events of social character, and subscribers had free entry to a series of evening open-air concerts or promenades, which began in 1833. Music was provided by the bands of various regiments stationed in the town. The success of the promenades depended on the vagaries of the weather. In 1835 it was noted:

> The weather, during the summer, has been peculiarly favourable for the evening Promenades – they have consequently been well attended, and have provided a source of delightful and rational enjoyment.[36]

In the previous year the weather had proved less than kind to a social event organised by the Society on an extensive scale. In April 1834 it was decided to hold a Public Fête at the Gardens on 4 August as a means of raising funds. The patronage of the local nobility was actively sought for this event and the names of sixteen titled persons were included in the announcements. Entrance was by ticket, at ten shillings for adults and five shillings for children, and the arrangements included entertainments by a theatrical company, musical interludes by the band of the Lancers, a breakfast and dancing. The proceedings of this novel and attractive entertainment were fully reported in *Aris's Gazette* on 11 August. The weather, however, did not augur well from the start:

> The morning was unfortunately lowering, and many parties from a distance were in consequence deterred from venturing. Notwithstanding, however, a numerous company were assembled about two o'clock, and among the most distinguished were – the Earl and Countess of Dartmouth and party, the Earl and Countess of Bradford and family, Sir Edward and Lady Hartopp, Sir E.D. Scott, the Rev. Chancellor and Lady Charlotte Law, the Hon. Miss Ward, a party from Lord Grey of Groby's at Enville, Mrs Taylor, Mr and Mrs James Taylor, Col. Thorn, Major Barton and the Officers of the Lancers, in addition to some of the most respectable families from the surrounding towns and district ... On the arrival of the Noble President's party, the company repaired to the spacious booth, where the repast was elegantly laid out by Mr Dee, the whole extent of the temporary erection being occupied with eleven amply stored tables, comprising every thing in season that could tempt the appetite, and including fruit of all descriptions ... At the close of the breakfast, 'Non Nobis, Domine' was sung, and the company immediately afterwards adjourned to the Dancing-room, where the Quadrille Band struck up, and dancing commenced.

Others strolled about the lawn listening to the band of the Lancers followed by songs given by the theatrical company:

> The varied amusements were thus proceeding, when they were abruptly and almost entirely put an end to about six o'clock, by a heavy fall of rain, which quickly drove the company under shelter, where they were compelled to remain until enabled to gradually disperse.

As the newspaper predicted 'the Society cannot have gained much', and in fact the profits amounted to only £31, and the ex-

1 Frontispiece to *The Floral Cabinet*, Vol. I, 1837. From the left-hand urn clockwise, the specimens shown are *Cattleya labiata, Delphinium divaricatum, Macrochilus fryanus, Ipomoea horsfalliae, Cycnoches loddigesii, Delphinium divaricatum* (again) and *Aethionema membranaceum. Macrochilus fryanus* was presented to the Birmingham Botanical Gardens by E.W. Fry, a partner of the Birmingham mercantile business of Fry and Compton, who was resident in Rio de Janeiro, Brazil.   Photo: Simon Restorick.

2 *Hibiscus cameronii,* named by Knowles and Westcott in honour of David Cameron, the Gardens' first curator. This plant was introduced into Britain in 1837 and was raised at the Birmingham Botanical Gardens from seeds donated by the Reverend John Angell James who had received them from missionaries in Madagascar. A plant was subsequently sent by David Cameron to Kew and was used for this hand-coloured lithograph by W. H. Fitch in *Curtis's Botanical Magazine,* 1842 (plate 3936). Photo: Simon Restorick.

3 (opposite) *Tanghinia veneniflua,* the poison flowing Tanghin, was raised at the Birmingham Botanical Gardens from cuttings presented by Charles Barclay of Bury Hill, who had received seeds from Madagascar collected by Charles Telfair. This illustration is from *The Floral Cabinet,* Vol. II, 1838. Photo: Simon Restorick.

3936

W.Fitch.del.

Pub. by S. Curtis Glazenwood Essex Apr.l 1.1842.

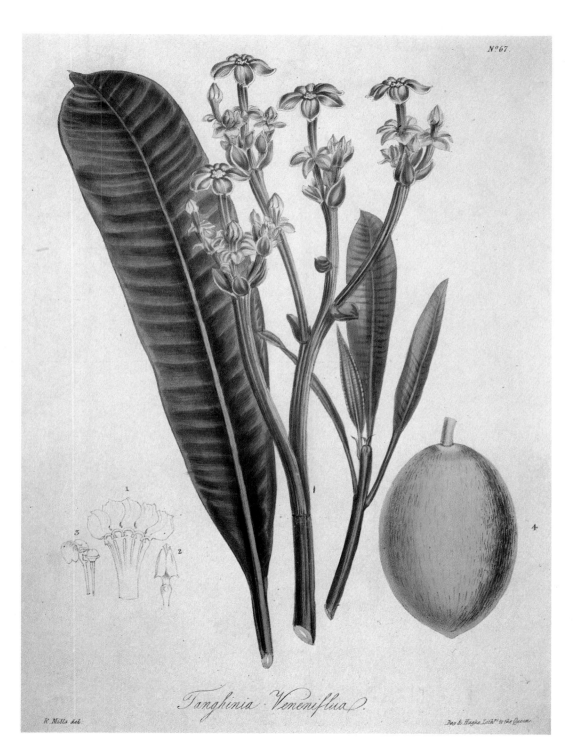

Tanghinia Veneniflua.

R. Mills del.   Day & Hagke Lith^t to the Queen.

Miss Cameron del.

4 *Tradescantia spicata* was introduced into Britain in 1837, having been donated to the Birmingham Botanical Gardens by George Barker, on whose behalf it was collected by Mr. Ross. This illustration from *The Floral Cabinet,* Vol. III, 1839, is by Frances Cameron, the daughter of the Curator. Photo: Simon Restorick.

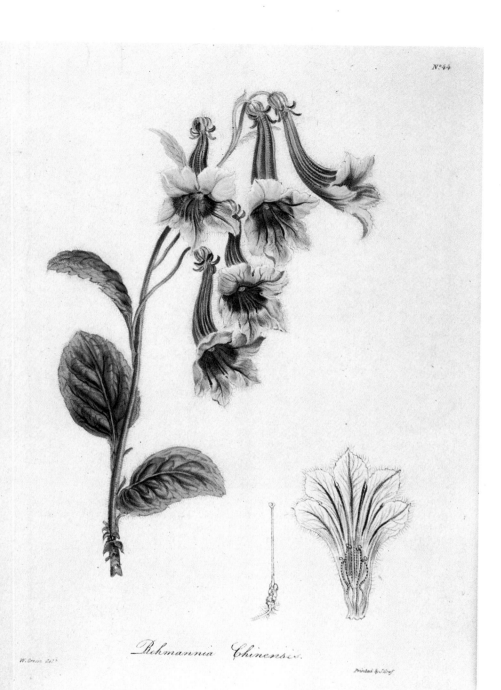

Rehmannia Chinensis.

5 *Rehmannia chinensis,* a native of China, was among a large consignment of plants sent to the Birmingham Botanical Gardens in 1835 by Mr. Otto, curator of the Royal Botanic Garden, Berlin. This illustration is from *The Floral Cabinet,* Vol. I, 1837. Photo: Simon Restorick.

6　The Domed Conservatory and the Lily House, 1854. The Lily House, designed by
Charles Edge, was erected in 1852, in order to display a specimen of *Victoria amazonica*
donated to the Birmingham Botanical and Horticultural Society by Joseph Paxton,
head gardener to the Duke of Devonshire at Chatsworth.

7 *Victoria amazonica* in its natural habitat. This hand-coloured lithograph by W. H. Fitch appeared in *Curtis's Botanical Magazine* in 1846 (plate 4275). Photo: Simon Restorick.

8   The Terrace and Domed Conservatory, *c.*1855, from a watercolour in the album of
Elizabeth Phipson, who lived next door to the Gardens at Westbourne.   Photo:
Simon Restorick.

periment was not repeated.

However, the Gardens were the setting for a private entertainment given in 1839 when the Society granted exclusive use of the Gardens to the British Association for the Advancement of Science for a déjeuner for members of the Association attending a conference in Birmingham. A special exhibition of flowers, fruits and vegetables was organised by the Society, and the British Association made a donation of £53 towards the expenses incurred.

Although the Birmingham Botanic Gardens achieved a standard of excellence that placed them in the forefront of similar institutions in the country, the Society had considerable financial problems from the outset. When Loudon accepted the commission to landscape the gardens in 1831 the Society had succeeded in raising a share capital of £3,000. The costs incurred in the layout, however, had amounted to just over £5,000.[37]

In contrast to Birmingham, proposals to form botanic gardens in other urban centres had attracted considerably greater financial support. The scheme for a botanic garden in Manchester proposed in 1827 had attracted a share capital of £12,000 'raised in a few days', and the Sheffield project of 1833 had started with £10,000, to which facts Mr Knowles drew the attention of the Birmingham shareholders in 1834.

The level of expenditure on two botanic gardens opened soon after the Birmingham Gardens was also considerably higher. The Regent's Park Botanic Garden of the Royal Botanic Society of London had cost £12,000 to lay out in 1838, and the gardens of the Leeds Zoological and Botanical Society, opened in 1840, had cost £11,000. In Leeds, however, the level of expenditure was out of all proportion to the income of the Society, and the Gardens were closed eight years later.

The BBHS therefore began operations with a deficit of £2,000. The annual income averaged £900, of which three-quarters was raised from subscriptions and the remainder from the sale of plants, fruit and vegetables, and by exhibition receipts and entrance fees, though the latter rarely exceeded £15 p.a. Out of the expenses of maintaining the Gardens, the payment of a Curator's salary and of wages to the lodge-keeper, subscription collector and workmen accounted for half the annual expenditure, and the rest was taken up by the annual ground rent, exhibition expenses, fuel and materials and interest payments, leaving no surplus to pay off the debt. In 1835 the Committee decided to issue a further 600 shares at three guineas to existing shareholders, and by October 1836 400 had been subscribed and the debt reduced. In 1840 the annual subscription was raised from one guinea to £1.11.6d, but this resulted in only a minimal increase in the income from annual subscriptions. By 1844 new financial problems were looming on the horizon. Lord Calthorpe's ninety-nine-year lease to the Society granted in 1831 had been for an annual rental of £115, which was to be increased to £180 from 1848. This increase the Society could ill afford and could, if implemented, have led to the collapse of the Society.

In March 1844 the Committee considered granting building leases on the lower portions of the Gardens and at the same time approached Lord Calthorpe's agent to see whether the terms of the lease could be renegotiated. Lord Calthorpe proved to be sympathetic to the Society's financial problems and consented to an amendment to the lease. The Society agreed to return six acres of the Gardens to Lord Calthorpe, and was henceforth to pay an annual ground rent of £41 for the remaining ten acres, Lord Calthorpe foregoing for his lifetime the ground rent of £50 for the house. The agreement was conditional on the Society's guarantee not to sub-let any of the land for building or to build on it themselves.

This led to a substantial modification to the layout of the Gardens by the loss of the six acres occupied by the reserve ground, agricultural garden and orchard and fruit

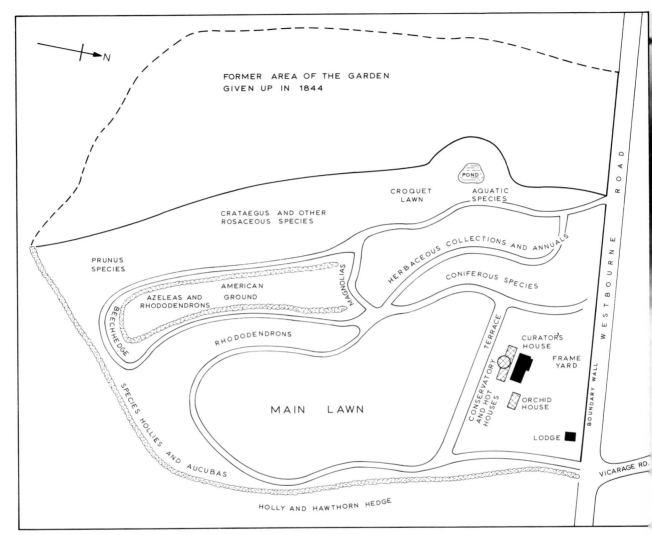

Conjectural plan of the Birmingham Botanical Gardens, *c.* 1845.

garden. Some specimens from the botanical areas in the lower part of the gardens were replanted in new beds formed in the lawn. The same year also saw important changes in the policy of admissions to the Gardens. From the time of its opening strangers had been admitted on payment of 1/-, and students of the Birmingham Royal School of Medicine had also been granted access to the Gardens. Entrance had been subsequently granted to the pupils of local boarding schools for an annual payment of 5/- in 1833 and gratuitous entrance granted to the pupils of Charity Schools in 1842. In October 1844 the AGM approved a resolution that henceforth the Gardens should be open to the working classes on Mondays and Tuesdays on payment of a penny per person. However, in order that these visitors should cause the minimum of disruption to what was essentially a Botanic Garden for the instruction and recreation of middle-class subscribers, the penny visitors were excluded from the hothouses and picnic baskets, games on the lawn and smoking were forbidden. In addition two policemen were to be on duty in case of any disturbance.

At this date the botanic gardens of other urban centres varied considerably in their policies regarding working-class visitors. Entrance to the Glasgow Botanic Gardens was generally restricted to subscribers and shilling visitors, though for several days in the summer free entrance was allowed to working-class visitors under the terms of a gift made by a local benefactor.[38] The Liverpool Botanic Garden, which by this date was owned by the Town Council, granted free admissions on Sundays and one week day.[39] The level of entrance fees charged by other botanic gardens effectively discouraged working-class visitors from regular visits, though public fêtes at the Sheffield and Leeds Gardens were attended by a wide cross section.[40] The Belfast Botanic Gardens had an entry fee of one shilling, though after 1865 a Free Admission fund was established to encourage working-class visitors.[41]

The BBHS was therefore notable in extending regular access to its Gardens to working-class visitors at an early date. This concession can be seen as particularly significant in the Birmingham area, as in 1844 there were no public parks and the town was rapidly extending in all directions, with working-class housing mainly concentrated in the central districts in proximity to workshops and factories.

2

The 'Ornamental' versus the 'Scientific', 1846-1883

The original intentions of the Society to run a botanic garden to promote the study of botany and foster horticultural skills lasted only seventeen years. After 1846 various pressures, largely financial, dictated a new approach to the development of the Gardens, and for the next twenty years attention was concentrated on the introduction of ornamental features in order to attract more subscribers, and the scientific aspects were neglected. In fact, this policy resulted in the placing of the Gardens on a sounder financial footing and allowed for a subsequent renewal of emphasis on the botanical and horticultural aspects.

The annual Report for 1845 had concluded with the following observation:

It is a source of great regret to your Committee, that not one additional subscriber, or Shareholder has been enrolled either from the Merchants or Manufacturers of the town; they however do hope that they will yet give this Society their warmest support, and not for the want of their assistance suffer such an Institution simply to exist, when by a trifling exertion on their part, it might be placed in a prosperous condition.

The need to attract more subscribers was the root cause of the controversy that raged in the following year and which came to be known as the 'Thomas Goodman affair'. Thomas Goodman, who was a Birmingham merchant and shareholder of the Society, informed the Committee that he intended to put a resolution to the next Annual General Meeting proposing a drastic reduction in subscriptions and that henceforth new members should be admitted on payment of an entrance fee of one guinea, with a yearly subscription of 10/6d and that these members should have the same privileges as the existing shareholders, and that they too would subscribe 10/6d annually.

The Committee viewed these proposals with alarm:

The proceedings of Mr Goodman are, in their opinion, calculated to destroy their most sanguine hopes, and ultimately to ensure the entire breaking up of the Society.[1]

They subsequently noted that at no time had the number of subscribers reached 600, and at that time numbered 353, so that it would be necessary, if subscriptions were reduced from their present level of £1 11 6d to 10/6d, to have between 1,200 and 1,400 subscribers to maintain the Society's income at the same level. They also noted their deep regret that Goodman had put his proposals before the public before bringing them to the attention of the Committee.[2]

This referred to a letter of Goodman's outlining his proposals which had been published in the *Midland Counties Herald* in November 1845. A general meeting of shareholders was called for 29 April 1846, but before it could take place Goodman addressed a further letter to the editor of the *Midland Counties Herald*, again putting his reasons for the proposed changes. In his opinion 240 subscribers had been lost to the Society 'chiefly by the high rate of subscription'. He also considered that the recent falling off in subscriptions was due to the introduction of penny admissions on Mondays:

> I doubt very much whether, of the 15,000 persons who were admitted last year, one-third were of the class of persons for whom it was intended. Such I know to be the impression upon the minds of some of the Committee, and that out of the number of subscribers amounting to between forty and fifty who left them only last summer, about two-thirds were supposed to withdraw on account of the facilities offered by the cheap admissions.

Goodman then repeated the point he had made in his earlier letter, that the Sheffield Botanic Gardens 'were at one period ruined by raising the subscription; they have since been restored to prosperity by reducing it to half a guinea.' He had since that time made enquiries about the policies of the Glasgow Botanic Gardens and had received a letter from the Curator, Stewart Murray, part of which he quoted:

> In 1843 and 1844 we reduced our rates, say a family annual ticket from 21s to 10s and a single ticket from 10s 6d to 5s, whilst the individual admissions were reduced from 1s or more to 6d. Every source of revenue has improved with these reductions.

The AGM of shareholders held on 25 September 1846 was unusually well attended. After the reading of the Chairman's Report and the Treasurer's Statement, the meeting proceeded to the business of Goodman's proposals. He then put forward the recommendations of a special sub-committee on which he had served, which proposed that the original share be reduced from £5 to £2 2s, and the subscription from £1 11 6d to £1 1s. This was seconded by Alderman Room, who observed that the more liberal they were, and the easier the payments were made, the more likely the Society's funds were to increase, and the resolution was carried.

The meeting then debated the proposal that every proprietor should have the right of admission for himself and family, and for eight more persons whether resident or not. The Rev. E. Bird then proposed that this should be amended to four persons,

and stated that in his opinion the Gardens ought to be made more attractive as gardens, and he wished to see more of the flowers of the season cultivated in them. Lord Calthorpe supported this view and further stated that he agreed with an earlier observation made by Mr Cadbury that the primary object of the Society had been to induce the pursuit of botany and horticulture. He thought also that, to accomplish this, the Gardens ought to be made externally as attractive as possible. 'Those who could hardly be expected to have a taste for the science being in the infancy of that enjoyment which he hoped they would yet acquire in greater degree, must be first attracted by what pleased the eye, particularly so in a neighbourhood like this, where there was a great number of persons who could enjoy the Gardens, but who had no opportunity of cultivating horticulture as a science.'[3]

The meeting then considered the proposal that a subscriber of half a guinea should have the right of admission for himself and two others. This was carried, with the amendment that it should be restricted to personal admission only. It was also decided that the price of admission for exhibitions be reduced from 2/6 to one shilling.

A discussion then arose over the problem of working-class admissions. Goodman's proposal that these should be restricted to tickets obtained from the proprietors was rejected. A further proposal that the privilege should be restricted to weekly wage earners was also rejected, on the grounds that it would be impossible for the lodge-keeper to distinguish such parties from others. Mr Luckcock drew the meeting's attention to the fact that Mr Cadbury had seen parties get out of a carriage and claim admission for a penny each and, although he had personally remonstrated with them, the lodge-keeper had had to admit them. Lord Calthorpe then observed that he hoped that the proceedings of the day had in some degree guarded against such abuses of the privileges referred to and that by reducing the charge for access to a smaller sum, they were, he thought, rendering the recurrence of the abuse much less probable. The question was then left to the discretion of the Committee.

A resolution that those who had forfeited their shares by non-payment of subscriptions should be allowed to resume them was passed *nem con*.

The immediate effect of the successful implementation of Thomas Goodman's proposals was the resignation of the bulk of the Committee – Howard Luckcock, one of the trustees, having tendered his resignation before the AGM:

> The proposed changes in the laws of the Society are, in my opinion, so objectionable, and so ill-calculated to promote the prosperity of the Institution, that I wish to withdraw from the official situation I have for some years had the honour to fill.[4]

The new Committee comprised those 'gentlemen with whom the changes originated', and included Thomas Goodman, Charles Edge, Thomas Clark, W.J. Beale and Joseph Gillot, though the three influential members of the old Committee – G.B. Knowles, W.C. Alston and John Willmore – continued in office.

Of more serious consequence for the future of the Gardens was the resignation of David Cameron in March 1847. The Birmingham Botanic Gardens had been singularly fortunate in their first Curator, and a resolution passed at the AGM of that year paid tribute to his activities. The meeting expressed

> its sense of the fidelity and ability with which Mr Cameron, the late Curator, discharged his office during seventeen years, and their hope that he may long continue to devote his talents and attainments to the cultivation of those important objects which have so successfully occupied his attention.

The actual cause of his resignation, however, gave some indication of the policies of the new Committee. Cameron had refused to comply with the Committee's instructions that many of the exotics in the Conservatory and hothouses be turned out and be replaced by 'showy' flowers. If this were done in March much would be killed immediately, the Society would lose the duplicates in the collection which were essential for the system of exchange, and new plants would have to be obtained by purchase.

What employment Cameron obtained after leaving Birmingham is unrecorded, and he died in the following year, aged sixty-one.

A restrospective assessment of the Goodman affair would indicate that there was right on both sides. It is evident that the exertions of the original Committee and their immediate successors had resulted in the creation of a garden that had an undisputed claim to be one of the foremost provincial botanic gardens, and the Committee were understandably reluctant to implement changes which they considered would lead to a diminution of its funding and ultimately to closure. On the other hand, the logic of Goodman's proposals was irrefutable. He had demonstrated that other botanic gardens had successfully escaped closure by a reduction in subscription fees and a consequent increase in income, and that the Birmingham Gardens would have to follow suit. The opinions expressed at the AGM of 1846 indicated that a number of influential people felt that the Gardens were too exclusive and that the Society was failing to make the Gardens attractive to those without specialist knowledge.

An examination of the Society's finances in the years following the reduction in the levels of subscriptions show that the new financial policies were successful, since only in one year between 1847 and 1867 did the Society operate at a loss. The immediate result of the changed rules for subscriptions was an increase in 1847 in the number of shareholders from 352 to 500, and new subscribers of one guinea and half a guinea numbered 214, which increased the income from that source by £150. In the same year the Society received over £400 in donations from the neighbouring nobility and gentry, who expressed 'considerable interest in the recent endeavour to establish this Institution on a firm and lasting basis ... and encouragement with reference to the system of policy which has latterly been pursued'.[5]

By 1851 the number of shareholders and subscribers had reached 940, and yielded an income of £840 compared with £629 in 1846. The income from this source continued to exceed £800 annually throughout the 1850s and early 1860s. However, in 1866, the Annual Report noted:

> The financial position of your Society is not satisfactory. By reason of deaths, removals, and other causes, your Society loses on average from fifty to sixty subscribers every year, and it is only by a constant and large accession of new shareholders and subscribers that the annual expenditure of the Society can be met and its efficiency maintained.

A system of life membership was introduced in that year in an attempt to pay off the mortgage of £500, but only four subscribers, including Lord Leigh and Joseph Chamberlain, took advantage of the scheme.

During the same period the Society enjoyed an increase in income from its penny admission. Initially this was an insignificant source of revenue, but the acceleration in the number of visitors, which will be discussed later, meant that by the 1850s the penny admissions were yielding more than ten per cent of the annual operating income.

In 1853 the death had occurred of the Society's first President, the Earl of Dartmouth. The Committee placed on record 'their grateful recollection of the kind patronage and valuable assistance which he has afforded to the Society from the period of its commencement'. This tribute was well-deserved as Lord Dartmouth had indeed been assiduous in his efforts to promote the objectives of the Society. Lord Calthorpe was elected as the new President, and the Earl of Dartmouth's son, together with Sir Edward Dolman Scott of Great Barr, Vice-Presidents.

We must now turn to the development of the Gardens in the years following the Goodman affair. C.H. Catling was appointed Curator in October 1847 after the resignation of David Cameron. Catling had previously been employed at the London Horticultural Society's Gardens at Chiswick and he occupied the position of Curator at Birmingham for the next twenty years.

The Committee stated their conception of his role in the Annual Report for 1847:

> Your Committee have impressed upon Mr Catling that it is their earnest wish to effect, by every available means, such tasteful and ornamental improvements in the aspect of the Garden as may render it more generally attractive to the public: but at the same time, it is equally their determination to uphold, to the fullest extent, the high character of the Garden as a scientific institution, which it had acquired under the superintendence of Mr Cameron – a reputation which, in fact, is not limited to this country, but is widely extended over the Continent.

In the event the development of the Gardens over the next twenty years centred predominantly on the introduction of ornamental features, and the scientific aspects suffered considerable neglect, leading to a marked decline in the reputation of the Gardens. Initially, however, Catling was successful in fulfilling the Committee's dual requirements. In 1849, while it was reported that the Gardens had been given 'additional interest from the introduction of a considerable number of attractive plants', the attention of shareholders was also drawn to the new system of labelling introduced by Catling and to the fact that the plant tallies now possessed 'the advantage of the name in full, protected by a glass front'.[6]

Many of the ornamental features introduced in this period were of a permanent character and can still be seen in the Gardens today. Soon after coming to Birmingham, Catling, assisted by William Lunn, the gardener whom the Society had retained to inspect possible sites for the Gardens in 1831, laid out the rosary in the area which is still used for that purpose, though it has been replanted several times subsequently. Shelter for the rose garden was provided by the boundary wall with Westbourne Road, and the wistarias which clothe this wall were also planted at this time.

In 1850 the Committee decided to go ahead with one of the features that had been included in Loudon's original design for the Gardens by installing a fountain at the intersection of the lower walks. This was designed and installed free of charge by Charles Edge, a prominent Birmingham architect, who was on the Committee of the Society. It consisted of a large classical bowl of sandstone with a single jet, set in a circular basin. The Annual Report for 1851 commented that the fountain had 'proved a considerable attraction'. It was subsequently altered in 1874 by the addition of another bowl.

Two years later Charles Edge again gave his services free of charge to the Gardens when he designed the Lily House. The erection of this house was prompted by the gift of a specimen of the Giant Water Lily, then known as *Victoria regia* and subsequently re-classified as *V. amazonica*. The lily came from Joseph Paxton, head gardener to the Duke of Devonshire at Chatsworth. It was then considered one of the chief wonders of the vegetable kingdom and, despite the considerable problems and expense posed by its successful cultivation, the display of this rarity became a matter of prestige and rivalry for botanic institutions in Britain and the Continent.

Victoria amazonica had been discovered in 1837 by Robert Schomburgk on an expedition to British Guiana sponsored by the Royal Geographical Society. Its characteristics were indeed exceptional:

There were gigantic leaves, five to six feet across,

flat, with a deep rim, light green above and vivid crimson below, floating upon the water; while in keeping with this astonishing foliage, I beheld luxuriant flowers, each composed of numerous petals, which passed in alternative tints from pure white to rose and pink ...[7]

Seeds of the plant were then despatched to Kew, but they failed to grow; and a second batch were sent in 1849, when three plants were raised, one being sent to the Duke of Northumberland and the other to the Duke of Devonshire. This latter plant flowered for the first time on 2 November 1849, and Paxton wrote to Sir William Hooker at Kew that the sight was 'worth a journey of a thousand miles'.

The Lily House erected at Birmingham in 1852 is a rectangular structure 60' x 36', with a ridged roof and a circular pool 24' in diameter. It was erected by Branson and Gwyther at a cost of £800. It was not completed in time for the planting of Paxton's specimen, however, and in the following year the Duke of Northumberland donated a second plant. This was planted on 17 May 1853, and produced its first flower on 16 August and a succession of flowers thereafter. A full report of its progress, published in *Aris's Gazette* on 22 August, concluded as follows:

Several other blooms are expected to open and persons who are desirous of inspecting this magnificent exotic cannot select a better opportunity of doing so than at present.

In 1854 the Duke of Northumberland again sent a plant but it failed to flourish and the pool was then planted with crimson, white and blue water lilies. At the same time a number of large palms and rare ferns were moved from the Conservatory into the Lily House. In 1856 Paxton sent another plant of the Giant Water Lily to Birmingham; this exceeded all expectation, producing thirty-five flowers. The Annual Report for that year noted with justifiable pride:

It is gratifying to the Committee (while at the same time it is creditable to your Curator) to state that it has surpassed in luxurance of growth every

The Fountain, designed by Charles Edge and installed in 1850. This view shows its appearance *c*. 1875. From Robert Dent, *Old and New Birmingham*, 1878-80.

specimen of this splendid plant that has been seen in the various public establishments in Britain.

The building of the Lily House, although it enhanced the prestige of the Gardens, had provided little additional glass-house space for ornamental plants, and from 1854 onwards the Committee in successive annual reports drew the attention of shareholders to the pressing need for more glasshouse accommodation. In 1858 Catling prepared plans for a new range of houses which would replace one of the existing lean-to houses and connect with a new conservatory in front of the Lily House, in a style in keeping with the existing domed conservatory. This plan the Committee felt would 'afford ample means for the better display of ornamental plants, while it would add greatly to the importance of the Gardens, and afford additional

pleasure to all who visit that interesting establishment'. They noted that they had no funds available for the project and appealed to subscribers for a donation of one guinea. This appeal met with a very limited response and only £250 was subscribed. The Committee, with justifiable caution, felt unable to proceed unless £500 was secured, and in fact the range was never executed.

Meanwhile other ornamental features much favoured at the period were added in the Gardens. Such were seats around two large oaks; rustic arches at the entrances to the American ground; a thatched arbour; and a sundial on the main terrace. A water-colour of the terrace and Conservatory, executed in about 1855 by Elizabeth Phipson, who lived next to the Gardens at Westbourne, shows how beautiful the

Gardens were at this period (see Plate 8).

Catling was also responsible for designing alterations to the American ground, which may have heightened its ornamental aspects but decidedly diminished its scientific interest. In 1855 about a quarter of the whole American ground was remodelled as a permanent area for exhibitions, and in the following year many of the remaining American species were dug up and their places filled by rhododendrons and azaleas which, it was felt, would have more appeal to visitors.

Considerations of the ornamental appearance of the Gardens were also behind the decision taken in 1861 to curtail one of the important privileges enjoyed by shareholders. It was announced that in the following year the annual distribution of seeds would cease 'as much valuable space in the Garden is devoted to them, which your committee think might be more advantageously planted. Such annual seeds being not only an expense to the Society but as they must of necessity remain in the ground until the seeds are perfect they become unsightly and as such detract from the beauty of the Garden.'[9] Although in the short term the features added to the Gardens increased its ornamental aspects, this was achieved at the cost of considerable neglect to the continual restocking of the collections. Less and less attention was paid to the raising of duplicates for exchange, and by the 1860s donations from other botanic institutions, commercial nursery firms and private collectors had virtually ceased, and what was received came predominantly from private collectors in the Birmingham area. The donor whose name appeared most often was Archibald Kenrick, a manufacturer of cast iron hollow-ware at West Bromwich. From 1859 he lived at Berrow Court, Edgbaston, close to the Gardens.[10] He was a regular exhibitor at the Gardens' shows, frequently winning prizes for orchids, and made many donations of orchids to the Gardens.

In the 1860s the relationship between the Curator and the Committee came under increasing strain. Although as early as 1854 the Committee's attention had been drawn

'Proposed' new greenhouse, 1858, designed by the curator, C.H. Catling.

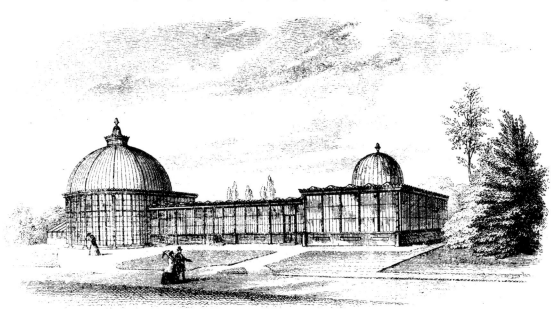

to the Curator's irregularities in the payment of the labourers' wages, he had been allowed to remain in office. By 1865, however, the neglect in the management of the botanic collections and in the general standards of the Gardens was more serious. In May 1865 some members of the Birmingham Natural History and Microscopical Society wrote to the Committee to urge them 'to take such steps as will make the Gardens better adapted as a place of study ... Many years back the nomenclature of your plants was much more fully carried out than at present although it has unfortunately been gradually allowed to fall into desuetude.'[12] They also asked that space be set aside for 'systematic illustration of the natural order of plants'; and though the Committee, hampered by lack of funds, could not do this, they agreed to spend £10 on the labelling of plants, to which the BNHMS added a further £2. It is evident, however, that Catling made little headway with the labelling.

The decline in the standards of the Society did not go unnoticed in the national gardening press, and in November 1865 the Gardens were the subject of some highly critical comments in *The Gardeners' Chronicle*.[12] The writer opened his remarks with some laudatory observations on the botanic gardens of Liverpool, Manchester and Sheffield – and continued:

> I strayed into the Birmingham Garden during the visit of the British Association to that town, but there was little to see there, though the Garden is not the worst as regards situation and arrangement. Perhaps, as usual, the money is the difficulty, but I did not learn. The houses are in a poor state; most trouble is taken with the bedding plants but, on the whole, the garden is unworthy of the town.

On 25 October 1867 the General Committee passed a vote of no confidence in the Curator and he was asked to resign. It must be said in justice to Catling that the Committee of the period should also bear part of the blame, since they had actively fostered ornamental projects and had only paid lip service to the scientific aspects, in contrast to the dedication of earlier Committee members.

The promotion of horticultural exhibitions had continued in the years following the Goodman affair, and these were held three times a year. The importance attached to exhibitions is shown by the formation of a permanent exhibition ground in 1855, making use of part of the American ground already referred to. Visual considerations, however, seem to have influenced the manner in which the exhibits were arranged. The Annual Report for 1855 said that the arrangements were 'strikingly novel and had not heretofore been adopted in the provinces'. Catling had apparently adopted the practice, introduced by Richard Marnock at Regent's Park, of placing exhibits decoratively rather than by their respective classes, for the Report commented on 'the tasteful and varied groupings of the plants and fruits'. This may have reduced the number of exhibits, though, to judge by the comments of one visitor to the June Show of 1859, the occasion was very enjoyable. Archibald Kenrick's daughter, Caroline, noted in her Journal for 9 June:

> Went in the phaeton to the Gardens' flower show not enough plants for that large tent, people very gay.[13]

Special exhibitions were also arranged, in conjunction with the free opening of the Gardens to visitors attending conferences in Birmingham; and these were organised for visits by members of the British Association in 1849 and 1865 and for those attending the Wesleyan Conference in 1865 and the Methodist New Connection Conference in 1866.

On 19 June 1851, the Gardens were the setting for a fête champêtre given by the Mayor of Birmingham, John Ratcliff, for the Royal Commissioners of the Great Exhibition and a number of distinguished foreign visitors. A party of 250 journeyed to Birmingham by special train and, after visiting the principal manufactories of the

Fête Champêtre at the Birmingham Botanical Gardens, 19 June 1851, given by the mayor of Birmingham, John Ratcliff, for the commissioners of the Great Exhibition. From the *Illustrated London News*, 21 June 1851.

town, attended the fête at the Botanical Gardens. Special tents were erected for the visitors, who partook of 'a very elegant déjeuner, the Mayor presiding, supported by the principal visitors and members of the Corporation'.[14] At the conclusion of the meal a number of healths were proposed, and the guests then strolled about the grounds and inspected the special exhibition of flowers and fruits.

Promenades continued to be held on between four and six occasions each year on Thursday evenings, and though on the whole they were 'numerously and fashionably attended' their success depended largely on the weather.

The working-class visitors continued to avail themselves of the privileges of entry granted in 1844, and from 1847 penny admissions were limited to Monday only. It is evident, however, that the more liberal terms of admission implemented in 1847 had been unsuccessful in preventing abuse of the Monday concession, and a significant number of middle-class visitors continued to visit the Gardens on that day. The Annual Report for 1851 noted that there had been 35,708 Monday visitors:

> At the same time it is to be regretted that persons moving in the higher ranks of life should still continue to make use of a privilege which is intended solely and exclusively for the working classes.

The number of Monday visitors continued to increase annually, and the Annual Report for 1853 noted that considerable damage had been done to the main lawn and borders 'from the indulgence in various games ... notwithstanding the strict orders issued by your Committee on this subject'. These visitors reached a peak between June 1853 and May 1854, when over 45,000 were recorded. After 1857 their numbers dropped as a result of Lord Calthorpe's gift of Birmingham's first public park, which was opened in that year, though the Gardens continued to attract over 25,000 Monday visitors annually. In 1865 the price of admission on Mondays was raised to two pence, it having been noted in the previous year:

> Your Committee, while anxious that the Working Classes should have full enjoyment of the privilege, are at the same time doubtful whether these large attendances are conducive to the Garden's well-being or advantageous to the Society.

This resulted in an immediate drop in Monday visitors, and only 9,789 were recorded for 1866. But this fall proved to be only temporary, and between 1868 and 1874 the Monday visitors averaged 20,000 annually.

The appointment of William Bradbury Latham as Curator in January 1868 marked an upturn in the reputation of the Birmingham Gardens. Latham had much varied experience in private establishments, commercial nurseries and botanic gardens, having worked successively for William McNeil of Wandsworth, the Wandsworth Common nursery of Robert Neal, Kew Gardens, the Duke of Devonshire at Chatsworth, the Jardin des Plantes at Paris, Messrs Parker and Williams' nursery at Holloway, and as head gardener to Lt. Col. Perkins of Birtley Hall, Chester-le-Street. He had a thorough knowledge of all aspects of horticulture and in particular the cultivation of orchids and exotic ferns. Although the Birmingham Gardens had declined in status there was evidently no shortage of applicants for the post of Curator, for Latham stated that he had been chosen from 'about two hundred

William Bradbury Latham, curator of the Birmingham Botanical Gardens, 1868-1903. From *The Gardeners' Chronicle*, 25 July 1903.

candidates'.[15] His first impressions of the Gardens showed the extent of their decline:

> The collection of plants was somewhat limited for a good botanical garden that had existed for thirty-seven years, and of trees and shrubs there were the remains of a fine collection, planted when the gardens were first made.

Latham's first task on coming to Birmingham, however, was hardly to his taste, and his comments showed that the Committee of the time were ill-informed about the nature of the botanical collections in their care. As early as 1835 an archery and croquet lawn had been set out, but in 1868 the Committee decided to sub-let a portion of their lower grounds to the Edgbaston Archery Society in order to augment their operating income, the Society being responsible for clearing the site and providing the necessary fencing and re-turfing:

For the formation of a large archery ground I received instructions from the committee of the gardens to destroy one of the best, if not the best, collection of *Crataegus* and other *Rosaceous* trees and shrubs in the United Kingdom.[16]

In his first year at Birmingham, Latham was able to effect a general improvement in the maintenance of the Gardens and also began the considerable task of labelling the specimens. In the autumn of that year work was started again on an ornamental walk and fernery on the south-east boundary of the Gardens, first begun in 1862.

At the same time the Committee decided that the problem of the lack of greenhouse space could no longer be deferred, especially as Latham's appointment to the curatorship had been followed by several gifts of rare specimens from private collectors and from the Botanic Gardens of Kew, Sheffield and Liverpool. The Annual Report noted that the present glasshouses were not only inadequate for displaying these gifts but were 'unworthy of the importance of the Society, and the Town and Neighbourhood'.

The Committee proposed raising a sum of £2,000 for the erection of a new range of glasshouses, and in July 1869 a local architect, F.B. Osborn, was engaged to prepare the plans. His design retained the domed conservatory, which would be extended. The lean-to hot houses would be replaced by new houses with ridged roofs, and a palm house erected in front of the Lily House. The following summer Osborn, accompanied by Latham, journeyed to London to inspect the glasshouses recently

The Fern Walk, completed in 1868. This view shows its appearance *c*. 1910.

Proposed new range of glasshouses, 1869, designed by F.B. Osborn.

erected at **Kew, Regent's Park and Kensington,** and by commercial establishments. Osborn's report, presented to the Buildings Committee of 27 July 1870, indicated what were then the accepted ideas in glasshouse construction:

> The ridge and furrow roof is now generally condemned and abandoned. Conservatories are as much as possible roofed in one span or with a central roof in one span with side roofs sloping up to it.
>
> All gutters are as much as possible done away with and wooden roofs in straight planes of glass are strongly recommended in preference to metallic curved roofs and bent glass.
>
> The houses we saw were nearly all heated by Ireland's boiler and hot water pipes and we understood that it gave great satisfaction and produced great heat with small consumption of fuel.

Osborn concluded his report with the observation that since his return he had made some new designs for the large conservatory which included the improvements in construction and detail mentioned in his letter. These are apparent in the re-design of the upper part of the Palm House and its roof.

Donations to the Building Fund at this point amounted to £1,200 and it was decided to invite tenders for the construction of the large conservatory. The lowest tender was submitted by Messrs Cresswell and Sons of Birmingham at a cost of £920, and this was accepted. The contract for the interior ironwork was awarded to P.D. Bennett and Co. of West Bromwich. Messrs Chance Brothers and Company of Smethwick generously agreed to supply the glass at cost price, and this amounted to £102.[17] For the heating of the Conservatory, two boilers were bought from Messrs Ireland of Manchester and the necessary pipes and fittings were supplied at cost by Villiers Blakemore.

The Palm House was completed by June 1871 to the entire satisfaction of the Committee, who noted in the Annual Report:

> They believe that no similar public erection (out of the Metropolis) surpasses it, in the completeness of its arrangements, the beauty of its interior, and the variety and value of its contents.

The final costs of the new Conservatory, however, had amounted to £1,634, leaving the Society with a deficit of over £300 in the amount subscribed, and it was decided not to proceed with the rest of the alterations to the glasshouse range.

The Palm House, erected in 1871, designed by F.B. Osborn and executed by Cresswell and Sons of Birmingham. From *The Gardeners' Chronicle*, 28 September 1872.

View of the Gardens, 1874, showing the recently erected bandstand and Palm House.

One major project was embarked on in 1873, when an 'orchestra' or bandstand was erected on the main lawn. This was also designed by F.B. Osborn and built by the firm of William Partridge of Birmingham at a cost of £368, of which £346 was raised by a special subscription. The Annual Report for 1874 noted that 'the position and acoustic properties of the new orchestra have been found to be highly satisfactory'.

Expenditure in subsequent years was mainly concerned with costly repairs to existing features, such as the enlargement of the lodge cottage, the rebuilding of the boundary wall and the erection of a new ornamental smoke tower, 50 feet high, at the insistence of the Calthorpe Estate.

One permanent feature introduced during this period was of value in strengthening the scientific aspects of the Gardens. In 1882 a portion of land in the lower area of the Gardens was fenced off and devoted to a systematic collection of plants. The expenditure in laying out the Students' Garden was shared by the Society and the Mason College of Science which was founded in 1880. The College was the gift of Sir Josiah Mason, one of the most successful of Birmingham's entrepreneurs and among the most generous of the town's philanthropists.

Mason College was situated in Edmund Street in the centre of the town, and the facilities at Edgbaston afforded by the Society formed a valuable adjunct to the

The Students' Garden, laid out in 1882. This view shows its appearance in 1908. From *The Gardeners' Magazine*, 13 March 1909.

teaching of botany. The Students' Garden continued to be used by the Department of Botany of Mason College, subsequently the University of Birmingham, for the next sixty years and was discontinued only when the University acquired its own Botanic Garden in 1945.

Much of the credit for implementing new developments in the period 1867 to 1882 lies with the Honorary Secretary, Villiers Blakemore. He filled the office from 1866 until he resigned through ill health in 1880, though he remained on the Committee until his death in 1883. The Annual Report for 1880 paid tribute to his efforts:

> During his secretaryship, Mr Blakemore, frequently at great personal sacrifice, gave his almost constant personal supervision to the Gardens and the works going on ... In addition to the work of general supervision, Mr Blakemore has conducted all the extensive clerical work of the Society without the expense of any additional assistance.

Villiers Blakemore was presented with an illuminated address recording the names of 114 subscribers who had contributed £110 to a fund in recognition of his services to the Society.

As already noted, in 1866 the Society was facing the prospect of a diminishing income from falling subscription lists and still had a mortgage debt of £500 outstanding. In 1867 the Committee set up a Special Fund towards the discharge of this debt, and contributions from Shareholders, Subscribers and Friends amounting to £720 were received. In the same year the decision was taken to lower the entrance fee from one shilling to sixpence on ordinary days, it having been noted that in the past ten years the annual income from this source amounted to an average of £17. This change proved highly beneficial, and in 1868 the sixpenny entrance fees yielded an income of £147. In fact the combined total of the sixpenny entrance fees and twopenny entrance fees on Mondays was an increasingly significant item in the annual income of the Society and in the 1870s provided, on average, 20 per cent of the

total. From 1867 onwards the income from subscriptions also improved significantly and rose from £782 in 1866 to over £1,000 annually between 1867 and 1883, doubtless due to the new vitality that was apparent in the mangement of the Society in those years. The subscription income provided, on average, 45 per cent of the total income. The remainder came from receipts from exhibitions and concerts, the sale of plants, the rent from the Archery Society and an annual donation of £100 from Lord Calthorpe.[18]

The promotion of horticultural exhibitions continued throughout the period 1867-83. From 1867 the number of shows was reduced to two a year but extending over two days. Difficulties, however, were encountered in attracting sufficient exhibits since the prize money offered by the Society was too low to attract distant competitors. In 1877, because of the continuing shortfall in receipts from visitors attending the shows, over and above the expenses incurred, shows were reduced to one a year held in August. In 1876 special prizes were offered to 'cottagers, artisans and amateurs' for plants grown in windows and for cut flowers, though they were discontinued after 1878. The Annual Report for that year noted, with a singular lack of appreciation of the problems encountered by the exhibitors to these classes:

> The Committee have deemed it useless any longer to offer Prizes at The Flower Show to Cottagers, Artisans and Amateurs for Plants grown only in Windows and for Cut Flowers, as the Exhibits in these classes were of the most worthless character, evincing that no spirit of emulation exists in that direction.

From 1878 onwards reports of the exhibitions were published in *The Gardeners' Chronicle*. As was noticed in one of these reports, the exhibits came predominantly from competitors resident in the vicinity of Birmingham, and were of a high standard.

For many of the wealthier Birmingham manufacturers and professional men, the cultivation of stove and greenhouse plants

The First Flower Show of the Season: 'Was there ever a devotee of horticulture so devoted, or an admirer of the beauties of flowers so single of purpose, as to make his way through the tents intent only upon leaves and blossoms and thereupon to leave the grounds wanting to see no more? The First Flower Show is dangerous ground for the young and hitherto callous heart, and not always safe to the more mature.' From the *Illustrated Midland News*, 11 June 1870.

had continued to be a recreational activity of considerable importance, and their success depended on the combination of a knowledgeable employer with the means to employ a skilled head gardener and to afford the high costs of erecting and maintaining glasshouses.

In the classes for orchids, Charles Winn, a brassfounder, dominated the prize-winners, and other successful competitors in the classes for stove and greenhouse plants included W. and C.E. Mathews, a Birmingham land agent and a solicitor respectively, Henry Heaton, the manufacturer of coins, J.E. Wilson of Albright and Wilson, T.W. Webley, the gun manufacturer, and A.J. Elkington, the manufacturer of electroplate. The specimens exhibited were those favoured at the period and included palms, tree ferns, crotons, alocasias, bougainvilleas, stephanotis, begonias, gloxinias and fuchsias.

The exhibits in the large plant tent were arranged in the ornamental fashion first introduced by Catling in 1855, and *The Gardeners' Chronicle* report published on 24 August 1878 commented that 'Mr Latham, the Curator, produced an effect which pleased everyone'.

From 1878 onwards Messrs H. Woodward and Co. annually presented a cup to be awarded at the August flower show, and other firms, such as Messrs Elkington and Co., Messrs Pembrook and Dingley, Messrs Norton and White and Mr J.R. Fitter were donors of cups in subsequent years.

The holding of musical entertainments in the Gardens was greatly extended in the years following the erection of the bandstand, which was completed in 1874. In that year, in addition to the summer promenades on Wednesdays, two vocal and instrumental concerts were given, and a band was engaged on each Monday in June, July and August. The Monday concerts attracted a large number of visitors, who were for the first time allowed access to the Conservatory and houses – 'and no damage to the property of the Society has resulted'.[19] This appears to be the first occasion on which the Committee deliberately set out to increase the number of Monday visitors. Doubtless the large attendance of visitors at the band concerts organised by Quilter in the pleasure gardens at the Aston Lower Grounds at this period had not gone unnoticed.

Concerts were also held each Saturday evening in the summer, but these were less successful and resulted in a loss. They were temporarily suspended in 1880 but resumed in the following year when shareholders' rights to free admission were reduced to immediate members of the family, with the result that the receipts improved. In order to introduce variety, the orchestra of the Prince of Wales Theatre was engaged in addition to the usual military bands.

Important as musical entertainments were in attracting visitors to the Gardens, these were secondary to the attraction of the Gardens themselves and the collections displayed in the glasshouses. In the years following William Latham's appointment as Curator in 1868, a standard of excellence was achieved that once again placed the Gardens in the forefront of similar institutions. Although the collections do not appear to have been catalogued at this time, a considerable body of evidence exists of the species in cultivation. *The Gardeners' Chronicle* published no fewer than ten articles on the Gardens between 1872 and 1883, and some of these reports were of considerable length.[20] In addition, the General Committee Minutes and the Annual Reports covering the same period provide some evidence of how the collections were built up. Although some plants and seeds were acquired by purchase, the majority were obtained by exchange or were new hybrids raised by Latham himself.

As already noted, before coming to Birmingham Latham had had considerable experience in the cultivation of exotics – in particular, orchids and tropical ferns – and this specialist knowledge was applied to good effect at Birmingham.

In the Conservatory or Palm House the collection of tree ferns drew special praise from all commentators. 'On fine days the superb foliage of the tree ferns is most beautifully illuminated by sunbeams', 'nothing can be more beautiful than the tree ferns at Edgbaston' were two of the comments in *The Gardeners' Chronicle* of June 1874 and January 1875, while the writer of the article in July 1883 noted that 'the fine collection of tree ferns in the Conservatory here is amongst the best grown of any (with which) we are acquainted'. The collection mainly comprised Australasian tree ferns and included *Dicksonia antarctica*, *D. squarrosa* and *D. arborescens*, the latter having been introduced from St. Helena in the late eighteenth century but being still rare in cultivation, and the writer of the 1875 article considered the Birmingham specimen 'unique in the Kingdom'. Another species from St. Helena grown at Birmingham was *Diplazium arborescens*. High praise was also given to the specimens of *Alsophila australis*, *A. excelsa* and *A. contaminans* from Australia and to the New Zealand tree ferns, which included *Cyathea cunninghamii*, *C. smithii* and *C. dealbata*. Several of the tree ferns were raised from spores by Latham, while others had been presented by Birmingham collectors, notably the specimens of *Dicksonia squarrosa* and *Cyathea dealbata* presented by Joseph Keep, a Birmingham merchant, in 1872. A tree fern donated by Henry Buckley, the gun manufacturer, in 1873 proved to be a new introduction, and the Birmingham Gardens were the first to

Interior view of the Palm House in 1872, showing a rich collection of palms, tree ferns and other exotic specimens only one year after the completion of the glasshouse. From *The Gardeners' Chronicle*, 28 September 1872.

exhibit the Californian Coffee Fern, *Platyloma andromedifolium*.

The Palm House also contained a rich collection of tropical ferns from Central and South America including specimens of *Adiantum farleyense*, *A. rubellum*, *A. tinctum* and *A. concinnum*, and a rare specimen of *Lonchitis pubescens* from Central Africa, together with numerous Australian and New Zealand ferns such as *Todea superba*, *T. pellucida*, *T. fraseri* and *Trichomanes reniforme*. The specimens of the Stagshorn fern, *Platycerium alcicorne*, were 'seldom seen in such size and condition'. There was also a collection of palms and cycads, such as *Cycas revoluta*, *Latania borbonica* and the West Indian fan palm *Sabal umbraculifera*. In 1872 Charles

Ratcliff donated a specimen of the date palm, *Phoenix dactylifera*.

In 1872 Latham made horticultural history by effecting a cross between *Dicksonia antarctica* and *D. arborescens*, which was named *Dicksonia × lathamii* in his honour. By 1882 this tree fern had a stem one foot in diameter and an immense head of fronds eighteen feet across.

In addition to these specimens there was a large collection of insectivorous plants including pitcher plants, some of which were

Dicksonia × lathamii, a unique hybrid produced by W.B. Latham who crossed *D. antarctica* with *D. arborescens*. This tree fern is still flourishing in 1983. From *The Gardeners' Chronicle*, 28 November 1885.

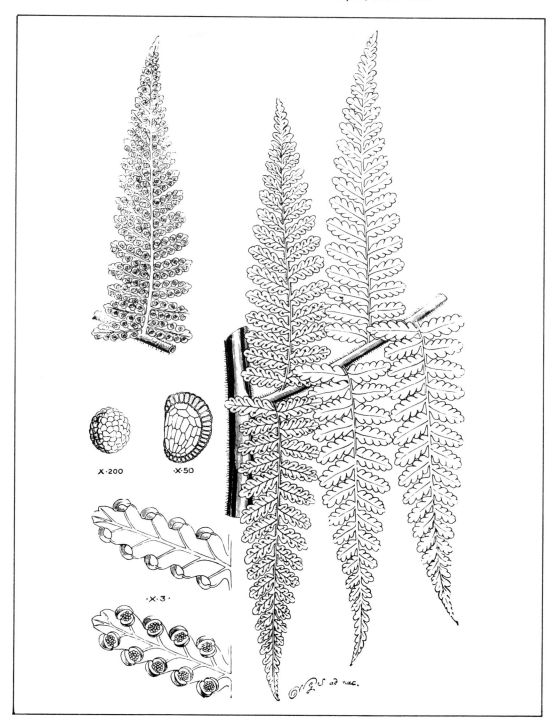

X·200   ·X·50

·X·3·

donated by J. Veitch and Sons in 1879, while others had come from the collection of A. Ratcliff. Colour was introduced by plants in pots, such as a lily from Central Mexico, *Dasylirion acrotrichum*, the guava *Psidium cattleianum*, *Camellia reticulata* and numerous orchids.

The Lily House under Latham's care was also filled with exotics. It contained a large number of palms favoured at the period, together with a fine specimen of the screw pine, *Pandanus utilis*. The roof was covered with climbers, skilfully trained on wires, with specimens of *Passiflora quadrangularis*, *Stephanotis* and *Allemanda cathartica v. schottii*, together with 'the little used and curious' Dutchman's pipe, *Aristolochia ornithocephala*, other bottle and snake gourds and the Chinese Sooly Qua cucumber. Suspended over the lily tank were baskets of stanhopeas and Christmas cactus with the Maidenhair fern – 'a new idea in basket furnishing'. The pool was planted with several species of nymphaeas.

The collection in the orchid house was also maintained in excellent condition and had mostly been assembled by Latham from 1870 onwards. Some specimens had been acquired by purchase, while others came from prominent local collectors such as Charles Winn and Joseph Chamberlain. Another important donation came from a Canadian merchant, J.B. Goode, who donated several specimens of the moccasin orchid *Cypripedium spectabile* in 1877. Latham also raised a new orchid by hybridisation – *Cypripedium* × *lathamianum* which was a cross between *C. spicerianum* and *C. villosum*.[21] By 1883 the orchid collection contained 250 species.

The domed conservatory and hothouses contained the standard subjects for greenhouse cultivation of the period and included camellias, azaleas and rhododendrons, together with orchids such as the recently introduced *Phalaenopsis* or moth orchids from the Far East and longer-cultivated angraecums and vandas.

While most of the species referred to were recent additions, something of the richness of the early collections seems still to have remained, and the writer of *The Gardeners' Chronicle* article of June 1874 commented as follows:

> Even at Kew it is quite possible to walk round and look in vain for many things we find hidden away in little asylums in the provinces, not because Kew is not spacious enough, though perhaps it may not be retentive enough, to contain the whole or to keep them when procured, but simply by reason of the diverse times and circumstances of the arrival of various strangers, many coming first through private channels, and being raised in private provincial gardens from seeds and bulbs ... Hence the pleasure of finding at Birmingham so much that in the fictitious sense is old-fashioned, as well as so much that is absolutely and positively new.

The gardens themselves were also maintained in excellent order and evinced many favourable comments. The writer of *The Gardeners' Chronicle* of September 1872 emphasised the qualities of tranquillity and variety they presented:

> In the Birmingham Botanical Gardens one feels in the country, far away from the din of commerce, the roar of trade, and the contentions of politics. Whoever chose the site ought to have a statue. And then the most has been made of it – Art and Nature have worked together to create a charming variety of terrace and dell, rolling ground and level plains, retired rosaries and sunk American garden, smooth archery ground and raw freshly exhumed rocks clothed with ferns and crowned with foxgloves.

At that time the fern walk was planted with a rich variety of hardy ferns such as *Osmunda regalis*, the royal fern, the oak fern, the beech fern, hart's tongue, aspidiums and onocleas, together with ivy. Its naturalness contrasted with the strong colours of the various bedding-out schemes, which were changed twice a year and in the spring might consist of 'a row of scarlet poppies followed by a zone of wallflowers, then concentric zones encircling a series of lozenge-shaped panels filled with myosotis or daisies, pansies or polyanthus', to be replaced by double-flowered pyrethrums, *Anemone japonica alba* and *Chrysanthemum* Etoile d'Or. Of the trees and shrubs there were fine specimens of *Picea nobilis*, *P. pinsapo* and *Thujopsis borealis*, a large collection of magnolias, specimen hollies and betulas, while an immense double-blossomed cherry dominated the bottom corner of the Gardens. In the American garden 'such masses of rhododendrons and azaleas, as one seldom sees' were an annual delight, though evidently not all the American species planted by Cameron had disappeared, since one writer noted a single *Andromeda floribunda* ten feet across and another commented on a specimen of *Hamamelis virginiana*, which though introduced into Britain in 1736 was now 'quite a rarity'.

Latham's main additions in the Gardens, apart from the ferns, were concentrated on building up the collections of Alpines and perennial plants. In 1881 many of the choicer Alpines were grown in the cool house, being considered too rare for the open garden. These included *Pratia littoralis*, *Campanula fragilis* and *C. raineri* – 'still very uncommon in gardens'. Undoubtedly these had come in a donation of 400 Swiss plants given by Charles Pumphrey in 1877. Other campanulas were included in the mixed shrub and herbaceous border that ran the full length of the outside of the American ground. Many of the herbaceous plants in this border came to the Gardens from the Rev. H.N. Ellacombe of Bitton, renowned for his cultivation of old-fashioned species which after a century of neglect were once again coming into vogue. Between 1874 and 1882 he sent four large consignments of plants to

Birmingham. Perhaps he was the donor of *Tropaeolum speciosum*, the flame creeper, which in August 1881 was 'struggling to regain its position owing to some diligent weeder having mistaken it for bindweed or some such pest'. In July 1883 an article in *The Gardeners' Chronicle* noted that among 'the general favourites (which) thrive and bloom here' were the following species: *Thalictrum aquilegifolium*, *Rheum palmatum*, *Orobus lathyroides*, *Asphodelus ramosus*, *Silene maritima*, *Doronicum caucasium*, *Orobus lathyroides*, *Armeria maritima*, *A. montana*, *Veronica gentianoides*, *V. prostrata*, *Ranunculus speciosus*, *Anthericum liliastrum*, double and single *Zinnias*, and *Pyrethrums*, double and single.

Another conspicuous feature of this border was the large numbers of irises, especially the bearded type. The writer of *The Gardeners' Chronicle* article of July 1883 remarked:

> It seems strange that these, the hardiest of hardy plants, are not more generally grown than at present ... for they go on increasing in size and strength for years with little attention.

Of the origin of the Gardens' collection of irises there can be little doubt. In 1877 a consignment of 120 species of irises had been donated by the Covent Garden nursery of Barr and Sons. In 1883 the rosary also drew high praise:

> Nothing could be finer than some beds in the Rose Garden, so full of flowers were they as to completely hide the leaves.

3

Developments and Diversification
1884-1913

At the start of the period covered by this chapter the Society had been in operation for over fifty years, and had succeeded in restoring the status of its botanic garden to that enjoyed in the early years of its foundation.

In the thirty years before the First World War this standard of excellence continued to be maintained in spite of financial difficulties, and a successful balance was achieved between the scientific and horticultural aspects of the Gardens and the provision of an amenity enjoyed by people from a wide social range.

Money for new developments was raised by appeals to shareholders and subscribers and though the sums contributed sometimes fell short of the required amounts, the money raised by this means was of crucial significance.

In August 1883 it was decided to appoint a special sub-committee to examine the problem of the existing glasshouse accommodation and to consider alternative plans either for extensive repairs and additions to the 1832 Conservatory and hothouses or for an entirely new range. The Gardens Sub-Committee had made frequent representations to the General Committee about the dilapidated state of the Conservatory, which now gave little protection in winter and was fast becoming unsafe. The collections in the Palm House and Lily House were overcrowded, and it was difficult to arrange displays of the finer and more interesting specimens in a manner that allowed the public to ap-

preciate them fully. In addition, although it was reluctant to undertake a programme of major expenditure the Society recognised that a considerable portion of the operating income was derived from visitors paying at the gates. It was therefore desirable that the Gardens should provide 'as much sheltered and covered accommodation as possible in order that musical entertainments, flower shows and so forth, which involve considerable trouble and expense in getting up, may be as far as possible independent of the weather and visitors take less account of its vagaries in deciding if they will pass the gates.'[1]

The Buildings Sub-Committee was chaired by P.D. Bennett, with Walter Chamberlain, a younger brother of Joseph Chamberlain, as deputy chairman and Hugh Nettlefold as secretary. Leonard Brierley acted initially as treasurer, and his place was subsequently taken by Frederick Ryland.

These men undertook the responsibility of preparing alternative plans, and also the onerous task of raising the necessary finance for the new glasshouses and to defray the outstanding debt. The sum required was over £4,000, a much larger sum than any hitherto raised for special projects by the Society, and a new technique in fund-raising was adopted. Lists were drawn up of those known to be wealthy, to each of whom the Committee addressed a personal appeal for donations. Walter Chamberlain, in particular, appreciated that the usual method of making a general appeal to subscribers would not raise the necessary finance. In a short history of the Gardens published in 1885 he recalled the difficulties encountered in 1853 when a general appeal for funds for new glasshouses resulted in donations of only £250. He wrote:

> Probably the Committee objected to undertake the laborious and by no means pleasurable task of appealing personally to possible donors, and these latter declined to come forward with open purses in answer to printed notices, a reprehensible but not unnatural modesty which is well known of collectors for public institutions in the neighbourhood of large towns, where appeals for pecuniary assistance to one object or another are incessant.[2]

Though necessarily time-consuming for the Committee, the technique of personal appeals achieved the desired result, and five months after the fund was opened donations amounted to £3,283. This sum, sizeable as it was in terms of the finances of the Gardens, was hardly indicative of the wealth of Birmingham at this date. By the last quarter of the nineteenth century the number of substantial citizens had risen dramatically, and the wealth of these men was of crucial significance in the initiation of a wide range of philanthropic projects, which included institutions of higher education, hospitals, churches and parks. Some of those most closely associated with these major projects were also generous donors to the Gardens' Appeal Fund of 1884, but others declined to contribute. Their refusal arose from the fact that the Gardens were only in part a philanthropic organisation, and though the working-classes were admitted at minimal entrance fees the general feeling prevailed that the Gardens principally existed for the benefit of a small group of wealthy Edgbaston residents. One correspondent, M.R. Avery, declined to contribute on the grounds that the scheme 'partakes very much of the character of private enterprise',[3] and the Earl of Dartmouth, the Society's Vice-President wrote:

> I should imagine that the lovers of horticulture in Birmingham, especially those who live in Edgbaston and its near neighbourhood, which my family have long ceased to do, will easily and readily contribute to the sum required.[4]

However much the wealthy residents of Edgbaston did benefit from the Gardens, raising money from them was no easy task, and one contributor, in a letter to the Chairman, wished him luck 'in the hard task of obtaining so small a sum of such a rich constituency'.[5] Some potential donors were activated by the desire not to be outdone by their neighbours and required to see a provisional list of names and the sums they had contributed before they themselves made a donation. Some refusals from individuals were on the more justifiable grounds that all their available resources were being devoted to other philanthropic projects.

The subscription list was headed by Lord Calthorpe who, in continuance of the family's policy of actively supporting the Gardens, contributed £500. Other substantial donations came from members of the Kenrick family, whose association with the Gardens has already been referred to, and a donation of £200 was received from Timothy Kenrick, £100 from George Kenrick and £50 each from William Kenrick and John Arthur Kenrick. With characteristic generosity Villiers Blakemore donated to the Building Fund the sum of £100 which had been presented to him on retirement from the office of Honorary Secretary. Other donors of £100 were R.L. Chance, J.H. Chance, J.E. Wilson and William Middlemore. There were thirteen donors of £50. These, in addition to the Kenricks, were P.D. Bennett, Walter Chamberlain, Joseph Chamberlain, Thomas Gladstone, Arthur Albright, George Dixon, G.B. Lloyd, Charles Beale, Frederick Osler, Herbert Chamberlain and Mrs Phipson. These twenty-one donations amounted to over £2,000, and the remainder came from 161 donations ranging from £25 to 10s.[6]

Terrace Glasshouse and Exhibition Hall erected in 1884, designed and executed by Henry Hope and Sons of Birmingham.

The Buildings Committee had prepared two alternative plans for the consideration of donors. One envisaged retention of the existing Conservatory, which would be flanked by a new promenade area opening on to four greenhouses and stoves. The other was for a range of four new houses in line with the Palm House which would have a promenade area and an exhibition hall at their rear. We have already noted the Committee's awareness of the effect of bad weather on visitor's receipts from the outdoor promenades. The holding of exhibitions in the outdoor area had involved the Society in considerable expenditure on successive marquees and was unsuitable for the winter and spring shows that it now wished to promote. Two other botanical societies had recently erected permanent exhibition halls, and doubtless those at Belfast erected in 1882 and Manchester in 1883 had not gone unnoticed.

In June 1884 the Society decided that the level of donations to the Building Fund justified them in proceeding with the second plan, and firms were invited to tender for the contract. It was awarded to Henry Hope and Sons, who submitted the lowest of the six tenders, at a sum of £2,400.[7] Henry Hope was responsible for the design of the new buildings on the ground plan submitted by the Committee, and the new range was built in a style that was in keeping with the structural and decorative details of the 1872 Palm House. The building of the new range took ten months and was completed in April 1885.

The new glasshouses and exhibition hall were opened on 13 May 1885 by the Hon. Augustus Gough-Calthorpe and Mrs A. Gough-Calthorpe, in the presence of a gathering of noblemen, MPs and major donors to the Building Fund. A special exhibition of rare plants was organised, with contributions from local nursery firms, including Messrs Vertegans of Edgbaston,

61

Hewitt and Co. of Solihull, F.B. Thompson of Birmingham and Hans Neimand of Edgbaston, and from leading local collectors such as Joseph Chamberlain, J.E. Wilson, Thomas Martineau and C.E. Mathews. Mr W.C. Stockley's String Orchestra was engaged to play from 3.30 onwards, at which time the public were admitted at 2/6 each, and the following day the public were admitted on the usual terms.

The opening ceremonies were described in *The Birmingham Daily Gazette* of 14 May 1885, and the reporter noted that the Society would now be enabled 'to develop new capacities both scientific and social'. He also drew attention to the problem of raising money towards the outstanding debt of £500, and appealed for a public-spirited effort on the grounds that:

> the Botanical Gardens are a public benefit, acting in a marked way on kindred institutions maintained by the Corporation for public pleasure and as such deserving the support of the public. Those who have most liberally subscribed have not been unmindful of those outside. The garden gates are opened to the public at a nominal charge once a week and on special holidays so that others may participate in pleasures which few at their own cost have produced.

Notwithstanding this argument the public's generosity seems to have been fully tapped, and no more contributions were received. In the next few years the Society was run at a loss owing to the outstanding debt and a falling off in subscriptions due to the general trade depression.

By 1891 the financial position had improved, and work was begun on the building of a glass-roofed corridor and annexe linking the entrance lodge to the Lily House. The Annual Report for 1891 noted:

> Your Committee consider that this new corridor forms a great addition to the Gardens, affording as it does an attractive entrance available in all weathers, and if they may judge by the increasing amount taken at the gates during the year, it is much improved.

Further improvements were undertaken in 1892 and 1893. These consisted of a propagating house – 'the absence of which has hitherto put the Curator to many shifts and straits' – a 40 foot range of frames, the extension of a watering system to the furthest end of the rhododendron garden and along the herbaceous ground and rosary, and additions to the lodge.

Although in some years the Society had been able to undertake minor improvements financed from surpluses in the operating income, it was clear that any further major improvements would have to be financed by another appeal fund. The Improvement Fund launched in 1893 had three objectives, which would involve expenditure of £2,000. The new Exhibition Hall had, in the event, proved to be too small for many of the concerts held in it, and additional accommodation was required for the successful programme of horticultural exhibitions promoted by the Society from 1891 onwards. The Society also wished to install electric light in the Exhibition Hall and glasshouses, a novelty which it was felt would attract more visitors. Funds were also required for the conversion of the old exhibition ground into a rock and Alpine garden, a feature that was increasingly popular in private gardens. By October 1893 donations to the Improvement Fund amounted to over £900, and it was decided to proceed with the enlargement of the Exhibition Hall and the laying out of the rock garden. Messrs Henry Hope and Sons were awarded the contract for extending the hall, which was completed in the summer of 1894. The enlarged hall was opened on 4 July 1894 when a concert given by the band of the Royal Marines was attended by over 1,700 people.

The contract for the rock garden was awarded to Messrs Backhouse and Son of York, who were one of the two most prominent firms of the period specialising in such work. The work was supervised by Mr Potter, the firm's gardens architect, who directed the Society's labourers. The pro-

The Hugh Nettlefold Alpine Garden, laid out in 1894-5,
designed by Hugh Backhouse and Son of York.

ject proved to be more expensive and more difficult than had been envisaged:

> The whole of the work was greatly delayed, and its cost increased, by the abundance of water which the site (overlying a sloping bed of stiff red marl) contained, and later on by a frost which for length and intensity, is without parallel in living memory.[8]

The rock garden occupied half an acre, and a total of 250 tons of millstone grit from Yorkshire was used. The final cost was £650. The rock and Alpine garden was formally opened on 29 May 1895 by Walter Chamberlain and named the 'Hugh Nettlefold Alpine Garden' in commemoration of his services to the Society. Although it took some years to reach maturity, it must be counted as one of the most successful improvements made in the late nineteenth century, and is today one of the most attractive of the Gardens' varied features.

Concurrently with the items of planned expenditure in the mid-1890s, the Society also had to deploy funds to unplanned alterations. Part of the 1884 range of houses had been attached to the ground floor of the Curator's house, with the consequence that the air used in ventilating his hall and sitting room and the room used as a Committee room and library had been drawn from the glasshouses:

> Year after year the Library Committee had drawn attention to the results of this upon the Society's valuable collection of books; and anyone who had occasion to enter the Curator's sitting room would have noticed the unwholesome atmosphere there.

Although the Society's finances did not warrant expenditure on a new heating and ventilation system for these rooms, this had to be undertaken as it was recognised that 'health and other considerations involved, were of far higher importance'.[9]

Although the scheme to instal electric

light first contemplated in 1893 was not immediately put in hand, from lack of finance, the idea was not abandoned. In 1897 a partial scheme was installed on the occasion of a Jubilee Fête held at the Gardens by the Institute of Mechanical Engineers in July of that year, half the cost of installation being defrayed by the Institute. By 1899 the electric mains had been extended to Edgbaston and the Society decided to install a permanent system, which no longer had to include the high cost of generating the current required in the original scheme. The system of electric light was inaugurated on 26 July 1899 by the Lady Mayoress, Mrs C.G. Beale, at 9.0 p.m. Musical interludes were provided by the band of the Royal Marines, who played a selection of appropriate pieces such as 'The Light of Other Days' and 'The Lighthouse Light'.

The Society recorded its gratitude to Mr Henry Lea, who had acted as consulting engineer for the project and had given close attention to the problems involved in lighting the houses where the high level of humidity necessitated special precautions and safeguards. The installation was undertaken by Messrs Verity and Co. Ltd. of Birmingham at a cost of £250.

Although during this period the Society was evidently experiencing financial problems, the caution exercised by the Committee in not taking out loans for improvements, and the generous response by the wealthy for new building schemes, meant that its financial position, though by no means encouraging, was not critical. During the same period three private botanical and horticultural societies experienced far greater financial problems and were forced to disband, the ownership of their gardens passing to local corporations or town trusts.

The financial problems of the Royal Botanic Institute of Glasgow who owned the botanic garden of that city dated from 1881, when the Institute was granted a loan of £25,000 from the Corporation in order to acquire the Kibble Palace, which they formerly leased, and to pay for a new range of houses completed in 1883. By 1885 the finances of the Institute were critical, and in 1887 the Glasgow Corporation as creditors acquired the Gardens, which were then closed. They were re-opened in 1891 under the management of the Corporation and with financial assistance from the University, and they have since functioned successfully as a botanic garden for the University and the City.[10] A loan also proved vital to the fortunes of the botanic garden owned by the Belfast Botanic and Horticultural Society, who borrowed £3,000 in 1882 for the building of an exhibition hall and extensions to the existing glasshouses. By 1895 the Society's debts amounted to over £8,000 and the gardens were sold to Belfast Corporation for £10,500. Henceforth they operated as a public park rather than as a botanic garden.[11] Reference has already been made to the high level of expenditure by the Sheffield Botanical and Horticultural Society in laying out their botanic gardens in 1833. In 1844 the assets of the first Society were taken over by a new Society who then administered the gardens. By the 1890s, however, this Society was also encumbered by debts, and in 1897 the Gardens were saved from closure by subscriptions and gifts of shares and a grant of £5,000 from the Sheffield Town Trust. In 1898 the Town Trust became the owners of the botanic garden, which were opened to the public free of charge. From 1951 the Gardens have been administered by the Sheffield Corporation.[12]

Although these three botanic gardens continued in operation with varying emphasis on their botanic collections, a fourth society was forced by a different problem to undertake a policy which eventually resulted in the closure of its botanic garden. By the 1870s the botanic gardens at Hull, opened in 1812, were clearly unsuitable for their original purpose, as they were now enveloped by the town, and the resulting pollution was affecting the collections. A new forty-acre site was acquired for the gardens in 1880, and a lavish programme of expenditure was embarked on. In spite of initial enthusiasm the number of subscribers proved inadequate, and by 1883 the liabilities of the Hull Botanic Garden Co. Ltd. amounted to £30,000. Part of the grounds was given up to the North East Railway Company, the major creditor, and by 1890 the remainder of the land had been sold to Hymers College.[13]

Although the Gardens of the BBHS were in the central area of Edgbaston, in Birmingham's most prestigious suburb, the considerable extension of industrial development in the town by the third quarter of the nineteenth century introduced the problems of pollution. The report on progress published in the Annual Report for 1897-8 noted the amount of time devoted to raising new hardy shrubs for the Gardens 'to make good losses caused to a large extent by the unfavourable atmospheric conditions of a neighbourhood so close to a large manufacturing town such as Birmingham'. It continued:

> The amount of filth left on everything, trees, shrubs, plants of all descriptions, glasshouses, etc. after one of our November fogs is something past description – our men last autumn were employed after one of these fogs scrubbing and washing the glass roofs of the plant houses, and it was with great difficulty the dirt was removed; some of our evergreen shrubs quite lost their leaves from this cause.

Nevertheless the Society does not seem ever to have contemplated establishing the Gardens on a new site further from the town. No doubt the Committee appreciated that this would involve a financial outlay beyond the assets of the Society. Although the plant collections were valuable, they were the Society's only asset, as the land of the Gardens was held on a lease and not owned. Moreover an essential portion of the operating income came from admissions at the gates, and this would have declined sharply if the Gardens had been moved to a new site beyond the reaches of the relatively inexpensive horse-drawn buses that conveyed working-class and lower middle-class visitors to the Gardens.

By the 1890s the Society was faced by new financial problems. Year by year the number of shareholders and subscribers showed a distinct downward trend, and the income from that source was gradually declining. At no period had Edgbaston had a total monopoly of the major wealth-holders in Birmingham, but in the period 1850 to 1880 it had contained the residences of a substantial proportion, who had constituted the majority of the shareholders. Gradually, however, many of them moved away from Edgbaston, attracted by the clean air and healthy properties of rural areas beyond the confines of the town, which were served by a network of commuter rail services and by improved roads for carriage traffic.

In 1880 the total number of life members, shareholders and subscribers was 1,049, producing an income of £1,135. In 1890 the membership was 922 and the income £926. Ten years later the membership had declined to 821, and the income amounted to £962. Between 1902 and 1908 there was a small improvement in the membership list and the income from this source averaged over £1,000 in those years. This fell below £1,000 between 1908-1911 but improved again slightly in the years immediately before the First World War owing to the attraction of the zoological collection introduced in 1910.

The fluctuating membership lists were a constant preoccupation for the Committee, who had to implement a policy of strict economy over repairs and improvements to the Gardens. One new source of income, however, was found during this period. Although the Gardens had occasionally been let for private functions, in 1897, on the suggestion of Prof. Hillhouse, it was decided to make this facility more widely available. A scale of charges was agreed upon and the attention of subscribers was drawn to the suitability of the Exhibition Hall and promenade area for private dances, wedding receptions, 'At Homes' and garden parties. Initially there was a slow response, as Edgbaston already possessed two venues which could be hired for private functions. These were the Edgbaston Assembly Rooms opened in 1885 and a suite of rooms at The Plough and Harrow Hotel, which were built in 1892. Gradually the income from lettings increased and in 1900 produced an income of £167, mainly as a result of the new system of electric lighting, as compared to £10 in 1897.

In spite of the financial problems experienced by the Society throughout the 1880s and 1890s, the new century opened on a note of optimism. The Annual Report for 1902-3 observed that 'the Society is once more at the commencement of a new epoch of utility. There is no sign that it is effete, no suggestion that it has outlived its purpose. It is indeed of ever-increasing importance to remind the people that to the rush and hurry of modern life there is no happier antidote than the garden, no saner or more peace-giving pursuit than gardening.' The problem of restoring the balance, however, between the Society's income and expenditure still remained, and it was decided that two lines of policy would have to be pursued. On the one hand, attention had to be devoted to 'a bold attempt to increase the attractiveness of the Gardens to subscribers and others by modernising the outdoor grounds', while on the other hand 'effort should be concentrated on making the Society's headquarters what they should be, namely a centre of information, as well as attraction, to all who are interested in botany and horticulture'.[14]

In September 1903 W.B. Latham resigned as Curator, a position he had held for thirty-five years. Much of the credit for restoring the Gardens' reputation as a centre of botanical and horticultural excellence was due to his wide-ranging knowledge and abilities. His prominence in the horticultural world had been recognised by the award of the Veitch Memorial medal in 1901.

Latham had also attracted a talented

Thomas Humphreys, curator of the Birmingham Botanical Gardens, 1903-1932. From *The Gardeners' Chronicle*, 25 July 1903.

work force, and several men who had worked under him at Birmingham went on to positions of responsibility at Kew. However, the best-known of the Society's employees was undoubtedly E.H. Wilson, who worked at the Gardens between 1893 and 1897. He subsequently entered the employment of James Veitch and Sons and was responsible for a large number of introductions from China, where he travelled extensively in the early years of the century.

The new Curator, Thomas Humphreys, commenced his duties in October 1903. He proved to be a worthy successor to Latham. He had started his gardening career at the Chester nursery of James Dickson and Sons, and between 1882 and 1892 had worked at Kew. In 1892 he was appointed Assistant Superintendent of the Royal Horticultural Society's Gardens at Chiswick, where he continued until his appointment at Birmingham.

In pursuance of the Committee's objectives stated in the Annual Report for 1902-3, a Horticultural Fund was inaugurated in June 1903, under the chairmanship of Prof. J.H. Poynting, with Neville Chamberlain as Honorary Treasurer and Prof. W. Hillhouse as Honorary Secretary. The proposed improvements would entail expenditure of £2,000 and would include rebuilding the Lily House, the provision of a new cloakroom, a tearoom and drinking fountains in the Gardens, and the replanting and extension of the herbaceous and shrub borders and rosary, which would be stocked with a large number of the best flowering shrubs and herbaceous plants, to increase the horticultural value of the Gardens to members and visitors.

Although donations to the Fund fell short of the target of £2,000, the money raised amounted to £1,400 and was sufficient to effect most of the improvements. In 1904 work began on rebuilding the Lily House, which was undertaken by Messrs Henry Hope and Sons. It included enclosing the pool with a retaining wall in order to bring the water level nearer the light so that the Giant Water Lily could once again be grown. In the following year improvements in heating the pool were carried out. In 1904 the rosary was entirely replanned and laid out in a formal design, and the herbaceous border along the eastern boundary of the rhododendron garden was widened and restocked. By 1905 work had been completed on the erection of cloakrooms near the entrance lodge, and further improvements were made to the ventilation of the Curator's house, including alterations to the Committee Room and Library so that subscribers could take greater advantage of the collection of gardening books and periodicals. The structural alterations were designed free of charge by Herbert Buckland, a Birmingham architect.

In 1906 the rhododendron garden was remodelled to contain two borders twenty feet wide with a central path, which gave greater ground room.

Although the plan to erect a tearoom first proposed in 1904 had not been prosecuted through shortage of funds, the Committee decided in 1909 that this was an essential amenity, and planned to raise the money required by loans from members. Refreshments had previously been available in tents, but these had required constant renewal and only provided limited facilities. The tearoom erected in 1909 was positioned on the terrace adjacent to the Palm House, and in 1910 it was connected to the Palm House by a passage and doorway so that it should be more accessible in wet weather and for evening lettings.

In 1909 the Committee, still preoccupied by falling membership lists, decided to embark on a new venture and introduced a zoological collection, an attraction proposed by Loudon more than seventy years before. Two members of the Committee, H. Howard Smith and H.S. Mathews, were responsible for initiating the scheme and making the necessary arrangements. An Animal Fund was set up which provided some money for the building of cages and enclosures. The majority of the collection was donated and comprised parrots, cockatoos, Java sparrows, ornamental water fowl, monkeys and a coati-mundi, together with rabbits and guinea pigs. C.R. Walter of West Bromwich lent the Society a collection of reptiles, an armadillo and an emu. In subsequent years the zoological collection was augmented by gifts of an opossum, a laughing jackass, ring-tailed lemurs and numerous birds and monkeys.

From the point of view of attracting more visitors to the Gardens, the introduction of a zoological collection was a successful venture. The Annual Report for 1911-12 noted that the income from subscriptions and visitors had increased by £500 in that year. 'It is quite fair to assume that this increase is entirely due to the new Zoo, which has given just that touch of living interest to the place which natural beauty alone was unable to supply.' By 1913, however, the Society had an accumulated debt of £1,600, and a Special

Appeal was launched to which there was a generous response, and a total of £1,300 was received in donations.

In the period 1884-1913 the plant collections were considerably extended by the exchange system and to a more limited extent by purchase. The excellence of the collections was due not only to the expertise and contacts of W.B. Latham and his successor, Thomas Humphreys, but also to Prof. William Hillhouse, Mason Professor of Botany at the College of Science, subsequently the University of Birmingham, who served on the Committee between 1884 and 1911.

Although in 1892 the Society announced its intention of publishing a catalogue of its collections, only a catalogue of the orchid and fern collections was actually completed, so that the numbers of species cultivated at the Gardens is unrecorded. Nevertheless a considerable amount of evidence exists as to the nature of the collections during this period. Between 1885 and 1912 the Annual Reports included lists of the species acquired in each particular year and rare or noteworthy plants that had flowered during the year. Articles highlighting plants of special interest were published in *The Gardeners' Chronicle* between 1891 and 1910[15] and a lengthy article on the Gardens was published in *The Gardeners' Magazine* on 13 March 1909. Considerable evidence also exists on the source of new acquisitions, since the list of donors to the Society published in the Annual Reports often named the species presented. Among the donors the Royal Botanic Gardens at Kew and Edinburgh figured prominently, as did the University Botanic Gardens of Cambridge and Oxford, the Chelsea Physic Garden, the RHS gardens at Chiswick and the Royal Irish Horticultural Society's gardens at Glasnevin. Single donations were also received from the Botanic Gardens of Lyons, Calcutta, Trinidad and British Guiana. Gifts from commercial nursery firms continued to be of considerable significance and the London-based firms of

James Veitch and Sons, Barr and Sons, Shuttleworth, Carder and Co., and Sander of St. Albans made several donations, as did the local firms of John Pope and Sons, Robert Sydenham and Gunn and Sons of Olton.

Important as these donations were, they were probably surpassed by the donations of private collectors, particularly from among the steadfast supporters of the Society, such as Joseph Chamberlain, Walter Chamberlain, Neville Chamberlain, Hugh Nettlefold, Charles Winn, W. Barwell, George Kenrick, Leonard Brierley, Prof. W. Hillhouse, A.J. Wills and A.B. Hollinsworth. The Rev. H.N. Ellacombe made five further donations of plants, and Gertrude Jekyll, the prominent landscape architect, sent two gifts of plants. In addition, several donations were received from members of the nobility, including the Duke of Bedford, the Duke of Devonshire, the Earl of Plymouth and Earl Beauchamp.

As well as participating in the system of exchange with these donors, the Gardens also supplied large quantities of material to local educational establishments, including Mason College, the Technical College, King Edward's High School, the School of Art and the Birmingham Natural History Society.

Subsequent sections will focus on some of the collections, starting with the glasshouse collection. In the Palm House the collection of exotic ferns continued to hold pride of place. The Catalogue of the fern collection published in August 1894 listed ten species of *Dicksonia*, three species of *Cyathea* and three of *Alsophila*, all tree ferns. In 1892 a writer in *The Gardeners' Chronicle* observed that 'in the lofty conservatory the Tree Ferns have grown marvellously of late years, some of their

Interior view of the Palm House, 1893: 'The Tree Ferns have grown marvellously of late years, some of their stems being 18 or 20 feet in height.' From *The Gardeners' Chronicle*, 9 December 1893.

stems being 18 or 20 feet in height'. There were 19 species of *Davallia*, 25 of *Adiantum*, 18 of *Pteris*, 5 of *Nephrolepis* and 4 of *Platycerium*, and the total collection numbered 328 species and hybrids. The specimen of *Trichomanes radicans*, the Killarney fern, was donated in 1890 by Sir Alfred Wills. This was displayed in a specially constructed case in the filmy fern house.

As already noted, the building up of the orchid collection had been begun by Latham shortly after his appointment as Curator in 1868. By 1893, when the catalogue of the orchid collection was published in the Annual Report, the collection numbered 309 species and nine hybrids. While the Birmingham collection was considerably smaller than that at Kew, whose catalogue of its orchid collection published in 1896 listed 1,725 species,[16] it did include 26 species not possessed by Kew. In a few cases we can trace the donors of these species. One of these orchids was *Oncidium intermedium* which had been introduced into cultivation in 1837 by George Barker, and had been illustrated by Knowles and Westcott in *The Floral Cabinet*. An article published in *The Gardeners' Chronicle* on 9 December 1893 quoted from Messrs Veitch's *Manual of Orchideous Plants* to the effect that after *Oncidium intermedium* had been introduced by George Barker, the plant was subsequently lost and had only recently reappeared in cultivation:

> The above extract is substantially correct, if we except the statement of its ever having been lost, since Mr Latham informs me that the plant has always existed at the Birmingham Botanical Gardens and is growing there still.

Other species had been acquired more recently, and included *Cattleya labiata dowiana aurea* which was among a number of orchids from Costa Rica donated to the Society by Wilfred Owen in 1888, and *Oncidium bifolium* and *O. uniflorum* from Brazil donated by Hugh Nettlefold in the same year.

Oncidium intermedium, donated to the Gardens in 1837 by George Barker. This plant was still in cultivation at the Gardens in 1893. From *The Floral Cabinet*, Vol. II, 1838.

Other orchids common to both collections were still rare in cultivation or were among the most recent introductions. *Cypripedium superbiens* from Java had been acquired in 1887 and had probably come in a donation of orchids from James Veitch and Sons or Shuttleworth, Carder and Co. *Cypripedium sanderianum*, collected in Malaya in 1886, had been bought in 1887 from Sander, and the rare South American orchid *Masdevallia davisii* in 1886.

In 1893 the Society bought a specimen of *Cypripedium chamberlainianum* which had been collected in New Guinea in the previous year. Latham raised a new hybrid by crossing this plant with *C. spicerianum* in 1897 and the new orchid was called *C. × deedmannianum* in honour of the indoor foreman, Charles Deedman.

The orchid collections continued to be added to in subsequent years mainly by donations, and further gifts came from Joseph Chamberlain's famous collection at Highbury, including a number of hybrids raised there, and from Charles Winn. In 1902 Lord Burton of Rangemore presented a collection of 200 orchids which also included a large number of hybrids, and in 1905 Charlesworth and Co. of Bradford presented a collection of 50 hybrids.

As already noted, no further catalogues of the collections were published, but articles in the gardening press highlighted some of the rare or spectacular specimens in the glasshouse collections. In June 1893 an article in *The Gardeners' Chronicle* commented on the specimen of *Solanum wendlandii* which was then in flower in the Lily House. This plant was a recent introduction, having been collected in Costa Rica and sent to Kew by Dr Wendland in 1882; Kew in turn donated a plant to the Society in 1891. The same article also commented on the fine specimen of the hybrid *Nepenthes mastersiana* raised by Veitch and Sons. This had been donated by them to the Society in 1886. A subsequent article in the same periodical published in August 1895 commented on several specimens in the collections seldom seen in cultivation, such as *Stigmaphyllon ciliatum*, the golden vine of Brazil, and *Crossandra undulaefolia* from the East Indies. The latter had been presented to the Society in 1889, probably from the Botanic Gardens of Trinity College Dublin. In addition the glasshouse collection included a large number of economic plants.

After the rebuilding of the Lily House in 1904 and improvements in the heating of the pool, the Giant Water Lily was again grown at the Gardens. In 1907 the plant was severely damaged by visitors and its cultivation was discontinued for the next two years, but subsequently resumed.

Seedling plants were donated by the Botanic Gardens, Glasnevin.

In 1886 the first plan of the Gardens was published. It was included in a popular guide to the Gardens written by the Honorary Secretary, William Southall, priced at one penny. With the exception of the Alpine Garden created in 1895, there were no major alterations to the grounds in the years preceding the First World War, though considerable restocking was carried out and several of the existing features were replanned to bring them into line with the recent developments in garden design.

Throughout the period a visitor who stepped out on to the terrace from the Palm House would see first of all the long top terrace bed with its collection of ornamental hollies, conifers and aucubas. On the sloping bank below was the main bed for spring and summer bedding out. Although the purists among garden designers, notably William Robinson and Gertrude Jekyll, had brought about a considerable decline in this fashion in private gardens in favour of a more naturalistic

Victoria amazonica in the Lily House, 1910. The girl on the chair is Thomas Humphrey's daughter.

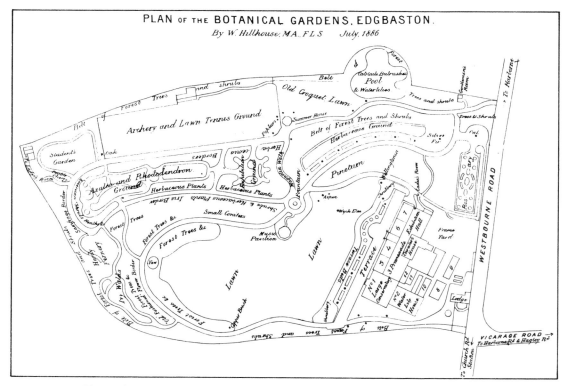

Plan of the Birmingham Botanical Gardens, 1886, drawn by Professor W. Hillhouse.

effect, it was still a feature of much popular interest in public establishments and was retained at the Birmingham Botanic Gardens in deference to public demand. About 20,000 plants were raised annually for bedding out. In 1909 Charles Curtis, writing in *The Gardeners' Magazine* observed:

> A different conventional pattern is worked out each summer, and while dwarf flowering and foliage plants are used freely to form the groundwork, the design is always relieved from flatness and monotony by the introduction of groups of pelargoniums, yuccas, agaves, dracaenas, begonias, fuchsias, abutilons, and many other effective and graceful plants.

Leaving the terrace at the western end the visitor would come to the Pinetum with its collection of conifers, including *Picea nobilis, Araucaria imbricata, Cedrus deodara, Pinus rigida, P. insignis* and *Wellingtonia gigantea.* From the top of the Pinetum a path led to the rose garden which was entirely replanned in 1904. It was laid out in a formal design of two long rectangular beds planted with old and new varieties such as Hybrid Perpetuals, Hybrid Teas, Bourbons, and species of Rugosa, Austrian briars and Moss Chinas. The two beds were separated by a central grass plot, which was subsequently planted with varieties of weeping roses – *Rosa wichuraiana* donated by Neville Chamberlain in 1906 and 1908. A hedge of sweet briars with climbing roses at intervals enclosed the rose garden on three sides, and on the fourth side the wistaria-clad boundary wall had a deep border planted with hardy perennials and chrysanthemums.

From the rose garden the visitor would

The Lily Pool, 1908. From *The Gardeners' Magazine*, 13 March 1909.

come to the Lily pool which was planted along its further margin with willows and poplars and later edged with wild flowers. Some of these flowers were probably raised from a collection of seeds of rare wild flowers donated in 1898 by J.E. Bagnall, author of *The Flora of Warwickshire*, published in 1891. From the pool the path skirted the old croquet lawn, subsequently used for games of cricket and later the setting for pastoral plays. From here the Alpine garden would be seen to advantage. The stocking of this garden took some time, but by the early years of the twentieth century it had assumed a more mature aspect, and contained many plants from a wide variety of sources. These included a collection of veronicas from Kew in 1898, species crocuses from Prof. Hillhouse in the same year, plants of *Anemone pulsatilla* from Messrs. Reamsbottom of Ireland in 1905, a collection of Chinese primulas given by J.A. Kenrick in 1906 and a collection of rare gentians from an anonymous donor in 1907. It also contained dwarf shrubs such as species of cotoneaster and *Salix lanata*.

The path that skirted the Alpine garden and led up to the fountain was planted on either side with a collection of magnolias which the writer of *The Gardeners' Chronicle* article of December 1893 considered the

The Alpine Garden, 1908.

The Fountain, *c.* 1900.

finest collection 'existent in any British botanical garden'. Judging from this writer's comments on the size of some of these magnolias, the collection included several specimens from among the ones originally planted in the early years of the Gardens, and listed by Knowles and West-cott:

> *Magnolia acuminata* is especially noticeable as a tall tree, and *M. conspicua*, *M. soulangiana* and other forms of *M. yulan* had their upturned branchlets tipped by exquisite vase-shaped flowers or glistening buds. Another rare old species with large and very fragrant flowers I was especially glad to see luxuriant and floriferous. This was *M. auriculata* ... it forms at Edgbaston a large spreading bush, 10 or 12 feet in height or more, and as much in diameter.

From the Alpine garden the visitor could reach the rhododendron garden. This was remodelled in 1906 when many of the rhododendrons planted in 1855 were placed in new positions and new stocks of the popular hybrid varieties were planted. Many of these hybrids were donated by John Waterer and Sons of Bagshott, Surrey.

In the spring, however, the visitor might choose the path that skirted the outside of the rhododendron garden, where from 1904 a new fashion might be observed. The grass banks surrounding the lawns of the Archery and Lawn Tennis Society were planted with thousands of bulbs. These were daffodils, crocuses and scillas, most of which were donated by Robert Sydenham

74

and John Pope and Sons, who gave more than 5,000 bulbs to the Gardens between 1904-1910. Among the bulbs were several new varieties of narcissus donated by Miss Willmott in 1905.

Continuing round the outside of the rhododendron garden the path led to the mixed herbaceous and shrub border. The stocking of this border has already been described in the previous chapter and several additions were subsequently made of popular herbaceous subjects. In 1893 Gertrude Jekyll of Munstead gave a collection of 28 species of paeonies, and in the same year the RHS donated 36 species and varieties of asters. In 1904 this border was considerably widened and stocked with ad-ditional paeonies, delphiniums, Michaelmas daisies, achilleas, aquilegias, phloxes, kniphofias, lilies and German irises. Likewise these plants were acquired by gift and the major donors included the Botanic Gardens of Edinburgh, Cambridge and Glasnevin, J.A. Kenrick, E. Miller Grundy, Lord Aldenham of Elstree, Earl Beauchamp, Bakers of Wolverhampton, W. Sydenham of Tamworth, Gunn and Sons of Olton, Kelway and Sons of Langport, Sander and Sons of St. Albans and Miss V. Willmott of Warley.

In the early years of the twentieth century considerable attention was paid to increasing the stocks of ornamental trees and shrubs throughout the Gardens, and the

The Rhododendron Garden, 1908.

Horticultural Exhibition, 1908.

new additions included recently introduced almonds and flowering cherries from Persia, China and Japan, Japanese acers, weigelias, *Daphne*, *Lonicera* and *Hamamelis*. The Gardens thus presented a judicious mixture of the old and the new, with features to attract all tastes. Charles Curtis, writing in 1909, considered the Gardens 'a miniature paradise'. He continued:

> Birmingham is well supported with parks and open spaces, but here is a semi-private garden, with landscape effects not equalled anywhere else within the City borders, with collections of plants that makes it a miniature Kew, and with opportunities for study and recreation not obtainable elsewhere within a reasonable distance.

This period was notable for the large number of horticultural exhibitions held at the Gardens. Some of the shows were organised by the Society itself whereas others were promoted jointly by the BBHS and specialist societies. In addition the exhibition hall was let to individuals and organisations for shows.

Though from the financial point of view many of these exhibitions were not remunerative, they were an important contributory factor to the prestige of the Gardens, and many famous names in the horticultural world of the time exhibited at the Birmingham Botanical Gardens.

The promotion of specialist shows began in 1891 when the Society joined forces with the Midland Carnation and Picotee

76

Society for a show held at the Gardens on 8 August 1891. The show was a considerable success and was held annually until 1916. The Annual Report for 1891 noted:

> In agreeing to a repetition of this Show, your Committee were largely influenced by the fact these flowers can be grown to perfection in the neighbourhood of a city like Birmingham, where many kinds of flowers cannot be successfully cultivated, owing to the smoky atmosphere.

In continuance of this policy the Society in 1893 organised a Narcissus Show held in April. This was the first show of its kind held in Britain, and the Annual Report for 1892-3 expressed the hope that 'in future years this Show may become highly successful in fostering the culture of what are *facile princeps* amongst spring flowering plants for town cultivation'. The judge at this first show was F.W. Burbidge, the Curator of the Trinity College Botanic Gardens, Dublin, and the silver medal was awarded to Pearson and Son of Chilwell, Nottinghamshire. In 1894 a prize for hybrid varieties was introduced, and at the 1895 Show this was won by one of the most prominent breeders of daffodil varieties – the Rev. G.H. Engleheart – for seedlings of 'Ellen Willmott'. A report of this Show in *The Gardeners' Chronicle* pronounced it 'the finest show in the kingdom'.

In 1895 the Society introduced a third specialist show for flowers suited to the neighbourhood of large towns. The Pansy and Viola Show was held at the Gardens on 29 and 30 May, and at the same time a Viola conference was held for professional growers and amateurs on the first day. The show attracted entries from all over the country, and silver medals were awarded to Dobbie & Co. of Edinburgh and James Backhouse and Son of York.

Owing to the state of the Society's finances, however, it was decided to discontinue the Viola Show in the following year, but the Narcissus Show and Midland Counties Carnation and Picotee Show were held as usual. In 1897, as a result of financial problems the Society felt unable to undertake the Narcissus Show, but permission was granted to Robert Sydenham, a prominent local nurseryman, to organise a Spring Show held at the Gardens. In the following year Robert Sydenham was the motive force behind the formation of the Midland Counties Daffodil Society, and from 1899 on this society promoted shows jointly with the BBHS at the Gardens. In 1900 a Midlands section of the National Auricula Society was formed to revive interest in this group of formerly popular florists' flowers, and competitive classes for auriculas were held on the first day of the Daffodil Show each year until 1907 when separate shows were held.

Of the three specialist shows the Daffodil Show was undoubtedly pre-eminent and entries were attracted from all the leading amateur and commercial growers in Britain. The shows were reported on in terms of highest praise in *The Gardeners' Chronicle*, and the reporter of the 1903 show stated:

> It is not too much to say it was the finest exhibition of flowers held in the country and much of its success is due to Mr. Robert Sydenham. To this show came experts from all parts of the kingdom. Miss Currie was there from Lismore, Ireland; Messrs. Hogg and Robertson from Dublin; and Messrs. Reamsbottom & Co., Geashill, King's County, had a collection of their glorious Alderborough anemones. The leading trade and amateur cultivators were to be found exhibiting ... and a large number of awards made to novelties by a strong committee of experts.

Apart from the Rev. G.H. Engleheart, two clergymen who were prominent breeders of new varieties of daffodils frequently won silver medals. The Rev. John Jacob of Whitchurch and the Rev. T. Buncombe of Ruabon gained several medals in the years between 1904 and 1914, as did other well-known amateurs, such as E.M. Crosfield of Bridgewater and W.A. Watts of St. Asaph. However, it is evident that the shows had encouraged the growing of daffodils for exhibition among local amateurs, and J.A. Kenrick of Edgbaston and R.C. Cartwright of King's Norton often won silver medals. A high standard of excellence was also evident among local commercial growers, such as John Pope and Sons, long renowned for bulbs, and the Kidderminster firm of Cartwright and Goodwin.

In 1906 the Society revived the policy of organising its own shows twice a year. The Early Summer Show was held in June predominantly for orchids, and a Midsummer Show in July for roses and herbaceous subjects. The arrangements for the shows were undertaken by the Exhibitions' Sub-Committee chaired by Neville Chamberlain, and the shows were held annually until 1915. They proved to be extremely successful and attracted a wide entry from leading amateurs and commercial firms.

The highlight of the Early Summer Shows was the classes of orchids, and among amateur growers two names dominated the proceedings in the early years. These were Joseph Chamberlain and W. Waters Butler, the Birmingham brewer. Joseph Chamberlain, however, had suffered a stroke in 1906, and though the Highbury orchid collection was successfully maintained for some years, Chamberlain gradually withdrew from competitive exhibitions. Between 1911 and 1915 the top award of a gold medal was won by W. Waters Butler, who exhibited many new hybrids raised at Southfield. Among commercial growers the firms of James Cypher and Sons of Cheltenham, Hugh Low and Co. of Enfield and Sander and Sons of St. Albans were frequent medal winners.

Commercial firms were also prominent as medal winners in other classes, such as Dobbie and Sons of Edinburgh and J. Randall and Sons of Shirley for sweet peas, and Gunn and Sons of Olton for roses, though a number of amateur growers from the Midlands and further afield competed successfully in these classes.

The entertainments organised at the Gardens throughout the period were very diverse and catered for all tastes. The Promenade Concerts held on Saturday afternoons in the Gardens throughout June, July and August were popular with shareholders and subscribers. Three of the concerts included vocal items, and were held in the Exhibition Hall. The band concerts on Monday afternoons catered for the 2d. visitors, who continued to visit the Gardens in large numbers but were particularly numerous on Bank Holiday Mondays, especially if the weather was fine. As the writer of an article in a local magazine put it, those visitors who might not 'risk mingling with that select crowd which paces the well-kept slopes to the music of that superior band' on Saturdays, nevertheless felt free on Bank Holidays to 'enjoy to the full the brilliant glory of the hothouses, stocked as they are with rare tropical plants, and while sauntering down the shady paths listening to the song of countless birds, try to forget that tomorrow morning will take them back to the stifling air of the engine room or the unpoetical monotony of the wash-tub.'[17]

To the musical entertainments was added between 1887 and 1890 a series of outdoor theatrical performances organised by Ben Greet of the Haymarket Theatre, London. The Woodland Players' programme for 1888 included a performance of *A Midsummer Night's Dream* given by limelight. Although the setting was clearly appropriate, the weather contrived to mar most of the performances. In 1899 Ben Greet again brought his company to the Gardens and presented a programme that included the forest scenes from *As You Like It*, the garden scenes from *Twelfth Night* and complete performances of *A Midsummer Night's Dream*. However 'the malignant fates which had pursued Mr Ben Greet's visits in years gone by waited upon him still', and the weather again spoilt most of the performances.

Nevertheless other companies were not deterred, and in subsequent years performances were given by F.R. Benson's Shakespeare Company, the Harcourt-Williams and Garnet Holme Pastoral Play

Bank Holiday Scene, 1908. From *The Gardeners' Magazine*, 13 March 1909.

Company and the Mermaid Society for the Production of Old English plays who gave performances of *Comus* and *The Hue and Cry after Cupid*. The plays were staged in the area of the former croquet ground near the pool on a permanent stage erected by the Society's gardeners.

After the enlargement of the Exhibition Hall in 1894, the Saturday entertainments were increased in number and ranged from opera to banjo concerts. Other entertainments included Monteith Randell's choir, the Euterpean Ladies Orchestra, musical recitals by Nelson Jackson, Leslie Harris and Willis Crisford, performances by military bands and instrumental and vocal concerts.

In 1901 a children's fête was organised for subscribers by the Committee, 'the "children" who participated ranging from some of the oldest members of the Society, to quite recent additions to subscribers' families. Marionettes, Conjuror, Ventriloquist, Pipers from the H.L.I., Punch and Judy shows, with Priestley's Bijou Band on the Terrace, and a coloured fire illuminated at the close, made up an eminently successful evening's entertainment.'[18] The success of the first children's fête led to its becoming an annual event. Out of respect for the English weather there was a Fine Weather and a Wet Weather Timetable of entertainments.

Although much more widespread use was made of the Gardens for private entertaining after 1896, some entertainments of a private character were given before this date. On 21 July 1891, the Mayor of Birmingham, Alderman Frank Clayton, hired the Gardens for an evening fête given for councillors and leading citizens to mark the visit earlier in the day of the Prince and Princess of Wales to Birmingham to open the Law Courts. For the fête the gardens were illuminated with coloured lamps and the evening culminated in a magnificent display of fireworks. 'A charming scene was produced, and the Gardens have certainly never been put to a more delightful use.'[19]

The Society also afforded access to the Gardens free of charge for entertainments given by philanthropic organisations. In 1892 the Gardens were used for the first time by hostesses for garden parties given under the auspices of the Walliker Society. This society, initiated by the Postmaster General, Thomas Walliker, promoted trips to the country and garden parties for old people from the slums of Birmingham. Although at first most of the garden parties were given in the grounds of private homes, the Botanical Gardens were to become an increasingly popular venue for these functions. Other philanthropic organisations were subsequently allowed free access to the Gardens when organising entertainments, and philanthropic societies who ran social fund-raising events were allowed to hire the Gardens on reduced terms. Although this did not come under the category of entertainments, the Gardens had a policy of free admissions for pupils of charity schools and from 1897 this privilege was extended to elementary schools.

4

The Gardens in War and Peace
1914–1945

Of the period of thirty-one years covered by this chapter, ten were war years when institutions such as the Birmingham Botanical Gardens had a considerable struggle to maintain their botanical collections and there could only be minimal general maintenance by reduced staffs. In both world wars the Gardens nevertheless offered to visitors a semblance of normality, an oasis of peace and beauty that contrasted with the bloodshed and violence unleashed alike on civilian populations and military personnel. The all-too-brief inter-war years witnessed the use of the Gardens for a spectacular number of entertainments enjoyed by a wide social range unprecedented in the annals of the Gardens. This was an extension of the rôle that had developed by the early years of the twentieth century.

The considerable expenditure on rebuilding the glasshouses undertaken between 1884 and 1910 was a lasting legacy for the first forty years of the century, so that little was necessary in the way of alterations, though the annual expenditure on painting, reglazing and general repairs was a large item in the Society's operating costs. The glass roof of the Exhibition Hall, however, proved less than satisfactory and leaked badly. In 1915 it was completely rebuilt. The Annual Report for that year noted that the reconstruction of the roof had been completed, 'though the cost has proved greater than anticipated'. The Report continued:

This expenditure will in the result without doubt prove to have been fully justified. For some years the leaky condition of the roof has been the cause of numerous complaints, but since its reconstruction several flower shows, meetings and entertainments have been held to the entire satisfaction of those attending.

During the period immediately following the First World War, however, the Society experienced considerable financial problems, and in 1924 and 1925 it operated at a loss. In 1926 the closure of the Gardens became a real possibility, and this was highlighted in an article in the *Birmingham Mail* on 8 June 1926. The writer noted that the Gardens had been administered for nearly a hundred years 'for the enlightenment and enjoyment of the community' and emphasised the continuing contribution of the Gardens:

Amateur and professional gardeners throughout the Midland area for many years have found much worth seeing in our Botanical Gardens, and have highly appreciated the assistance freely given them by the technical staff in the identification of plants and in the features of cultivation.

He also noted that although the City 'had public parks equal to the finest possessed by any municipality in the kingdom ... in certain respects the gardens at Edgbaston have landscape and horticultural qualities of a much higher class than anything the parks can show us'. It was to be hoped that the Birmingham Botanical Gardens would not share the fate of similar institutions founded 'with equally high ideals (which) have either ceased to exist, lost their distinctive merits, or survive only by State or municipal intervention'.

In fact 'by the date of this article the gardens of the Society were the only remaining privately owned provincial botanic gardens. Five years previously the botanic gardens at Manchester had closed, having been unable to find a solution to the serious financial problems occasioned by over-ambitious expansion in the late nineteenth century. Even the expedient of granting building leases on a portion of their grounds from 1917 onwards had been unsuccessful, and the Gardens were closed in 1921 and the remaining land developed for building. The inter-war period saw the closure of another botanic garden when mounting debts forced the Royal Botanic Society of London to give up its lease of a portion of Regent's Park in 1932 and the former Botanic Garden was incorporated into the public park.

The Society recognised that the continuing viability of the Birmingham Gardens depended on finding an alternative source of income over and above the income from gate receipts and annual subscriptions, especially as the income from the latter source remained virtually static. The Society did, however, possess one asset which had not been fully exploited commercially. Although the Exhibition Hall had been hired out for private entertaining, its facilities were limited. The income from lettings could be considerably increased if the existing buildings were converted into an entertainment suite. The numbers of private houses with facilities for large-scale entertaining had declined and the hiring of public institutions for private functions was becoming widespread.

In 1928 the Society took the courageous decision to embark on a programme of capital expenditure and launched a special Appeal Fund to enable it to carry out the extensive alterations and improvements to the existing facilities so as to augment its income from lettings. Donations to the fund fell well short of the target of £7,000, but by 1932 £3,600 had been received and the Exhibition Hall was refurbished as a dance hall with an adjoining lounge, the promenade was rebuilt as a supper room, kitchen facilities were provided adjacent to the Curator's house, and cloakroom accommodation was built near the entrance lodge. These new facilities, repairs to the buildings and extension of electrical fittings took the expenditure to £1,327 over the money received from the Appeal Fund, and this debt was discharged over a period of years. In 1939 the building of a new supper room was begun, which was completed in 1940.

The modernisation of the entertainment facilities did in fact prove to be a most successful venture. Whereas in the 1920s the income from lettings was providing an average of one fifth of the Society's income, in 1936 the proportion from this source had increased to a third, and by 1939 lettings were providing more than half the Society's operating income.

In March 1930 the Society negotiated a new 55-year lease from Lady Anstruther-Gough-Calthorpe, who continued to support the Gardens generously with an annual donation of £100. In June 1930 the Birmingham Botanical and Horticultural Society became a company limited by guarantee, which restricted the liability of the members to their guarantee of one shilling each, under the provisions of the Companies Act of 1929, and took over the assets and activities of the old Society. At this stage the Society set out afresh its objects and intentions. These were:

To establish, maintain and conduct a Society for the encouragement and improvement of Botany, Horticulture and Zoology and for scientific study and research therein and the diffusion of knowledge thereof and for any kind of athletic sports or games and for the instruction and recreation of the members of the Society, their families and friends and to acquire and maintain gardens, grounds, buildings, lands therefor and to provide facilities for social intercourse between the members, their families and friends.

To provide a hall and other suitable buildings and places and to permit the same or any part thereof to be used on such terms as may be thought fit for any purposes public or private and in particular for public or private meetings, exhibitions, dances, concerts, entertainments.

To hold or promote or to join in holding or promoting exhibitions, shows, displays, competitions or entertainments of all kinds (theatrical, musical or otherwise) in connection with the objects of the Society or for the furtherance of its purposes or for the benefit of charities or other like objects. [1]

This indicates the considerable extension of activities in comparison with the Society's objectives of a hundred years before, which had been primarily scientific and horticultural but had now a much more pronounced social character.

During the First World War the Gardens experienced considerable staffing problems through the loss of experienced men, some of whom joined the army and others left to work in munitions factories. Until 1916, however, the Curator was able by advertising and extensive enquiries to engage an adequate level of staff to run the Gardens at something not far short of pre-war standards. By early 1916 the recruitment of labour was proving more difficult, and the Gardens like so many institutions and organisations had to turn to a new source of labour and for the first time employed women gardeners. At various times the Society had up to three women gardeners on the staff, and although they generally lacked previous garden experience the Annual Report for 1916 noted that 'the Curator has every reason to be satisfied with the results of this experiment'. In the summer of 1918 the problem of garden labour was eased by the employment of boy scouts, who were engaged at threepence an hour and set to work at washing flower pots, weeding and removing seed heads from the rhododendrons and azaleas.

In 1917 the Society decided to augment its income by growing vegetables. The front glasshouses were devoted to tomatoes, the terrace beds were sown with beetroot, beans and carrots, and areas of the Pinetum were devoted to potatoes and parsnips. The long bed at the top of the terrace bank, however, continued to be bedded out in traditional fashion. This was the special responsibility of Henry Abbot, the head outdoor foreman, who joined the Society as a young man in 1871 and on his retirement in 1921 had completed fifty years' service with the Society.

During the war the Society experienced considerable problems from thoughtless behaviour. This was especially acute in the Alpine Garden where the plants suffered from being trodden on by innumerable children unable to resist the temptation to swarm over the rocks. In March 1916 the Curator was instructed to raise the existing fence around the rock garden and to 'introduce a strand of barbed wire as unnoticeable as possible'. In the same year the Curator reported that thefts of plant labels had increased when some visitors discovered that, if broken into convenient pieces, they could be used in lieu of pennies in the automatic sweet machines. The theft of plants also reached alarming proportions. This is not a problem to which the Society, any more than any garden open to the public, has ever found a satisfactory solution.

In the first year of the war entertainments at the Gardens continued at the same level as in previous years with a programme of two vocal and instrumental concerts, four programmes of recitals, band concerts at Bank Holidays, the Children's Fête, and two garden fêtes as well as private functions. The first effects of the war were apparent in 1915 when the Society adopted a policy of granting free admissions to nurses and wounded soldiers from the First Southern Hospital, which occupied the new University buildings at Edgbaston, the VAD Convalescent Hospitals, and to Belgian refugees. The annexe was set out with tables, and stationery was provided by the YMCA 'for soldiers desirous of communicating with their friends'. This facility was much appreciated, and the Curator reported that on 19 August 1915 a total of 421 letters and cards had been written by soldiers when visiting the Gardens.

In 1915 the Children's Fête was held as usual, 'but on account of the War without fireworks and other illuminations', and was

Wounded soldiers' hat trimming competition, 1916, judged by Mrs Philip Rodway. From
Phyllis Rodway & Lois Slingsby, *Philip Rodway and a Tale of Two Theatres*, 1934.

abandoned in the following year. The programme of Saturday evening entertainments was maintained, as were the Bank Holiday concerts.

Much voluntary effort was directed towards entertaining the wounded by such bodies as the Navy League and the British Red Cross Society who, together with the Birmingham Jewellers' and Silversmiths' Association, organised weekly garden parties in the summer months. At some of these garden parties, Philip Rodway, the Manager of the Theatre Royal, organised entertainments for the guests which included a 'Theatrical Costume Race' and a 'Hat Trimming Competition'. 'All these the men tackled with unquenchable optimism and good spirits, till the Gardens rang with their gallant and happy laughter.'[2]

By 1918, however, war-time shortages increasingly hampered such charitable efforts – the Annual Report for that year noted that 'several entertainments to nurses and wounded soldiers which were fixed to take place during the summer, had unfortunately to be abandoned owing to the difficulties of catering and conveyances'.

The inter-war period saw little significant change in the layout of the Gardens, though much effort was devoted to the restocking of existing features and, in the years immediately following 1919, to bringing the Gardens up to their pre-war standard.

The Annual Report for 1921 noted:

> It had come to be a matter for comment and complaint for some years that the condition of the grounds was not being maintained, and this was, of course, due to the extraordinary difficulty during the War period in providing the necessary labour.

84

Although the problem of the recruitment of suitable labour became easier, the Society's financial problems in the 1920s dictated strict economy in all departments. In 1926 the total indoor and outdoor staff was restricted to nine full-time men compared with a staff of fifteen employed in 1911. This made considerable demands on all the staff, especially the Curator, Thomas Humphreys. In addition the significant extension of the number of lettings in the inter-war period meant that a substantial portion of the outdoor staff's time had to be devoted to clearing up the grounds after social events, and the indoor staff had to be deployed on the necessary arrangement of the entertainment suite.

Although Thomas Humphreys' skills as a horticulturist were devoted to both the indoor and outdoor departments, the displays of flowering specimens in the glasshouses during his period as Curator were especially noteworthy. In the years 1919, 1924, 1925, 1928 and 1929 the giant water lily *Victoria amazonica* was again grown at the Gardens in the Lily House.

On 3 October 1925 Humphreys reported to the Gardens Sub-Committee that 'the *Victoria amazonica* has made excellent growth, and its beautifully fragrant flowers have been much admired by visitors and favourably commented on in the local press'. The plants were generally obtained from the Royal Botanic Gardens at Glasnevin or from Kew. In the years when *Victoria amazonica* was not grown, the pool was planted with nymphaeas including the blue lotus, *Nymphaea stellata*. The front show houses, the entrance corridor and the annexe were devoted to a succession of the flowering specimens favoured at the period. In the autumn these were chrysanthemums, Michaelmas daisies and phloxes, which were followed by begonias, arum lilies, coleus, primulas, cinerarias, salvias, specimen Indica azaleas, together with daffodils, hyacinths and tulips. From March to June there were displays of tree carnations, fuchsias, stocks, campanulas and spiraeas. In the summer these were

replaced by regal pelargoniums, zonal geraniums, petunias and sweet peas. The orchid collection was maintained at a high standard, and 1925 was noteworthy for the flowering of a specimen of the hybrid *Cymbidium diana*. The Society was congratulated on this achievement by William Alexander, the orchid grower to Sir George Holford: 'The Society has done very well to flower this specimen, which carried a spike over four feet in length with twenty-eight fully developed flowers.'[1] In 1927 the plant made horticultural history by producing a spike with forty-three flowers.

In 1926 the orchid collection was supplemented by specimens of hardy British orchids, several of which were donated by C.W.K. Wallis, who was a member of the General Committee from 1898 until 1942. Orchids were also donated by Neville Chamberlain, who had inherited his father's interest in growing these plants. He had a long association with the Gardens, which was marked by his election to the position of Vice-President of the Society in 1932 which he held until his death in 1940.

Thomas Humphreys continued as Curator until his death in October 1932, having occupied the position for twenty-nine years. The Gardens Sub-Committee placed on record 'their appreciation of his great technical knowledge, his energy and ability, and his readiness to help all enquirers'.

In the interests of economy the decision was taken not to appoint a successor. This put much additional work on to the shoulders of the Gardens Sub-Committee, the Chairman of the General Committee, and the foremen of the indoor and outdoor departments, who had to divide the duties of a curator among themselves. Two lady members of the Gardens Sub-Committee – Mrs Owen Thompson and Mrs Byng Kenrick – played a notable role in designing alterations, including an extension to the rock garden and replanning of the rose garden. Mr E.R. Johnson, who held the office of Gate Keeper, was appointed as Manager with responsibility for the lettings and day-to-day administration.

In 1935 there was a reduction in the orchid collection, and considerable numbers of the cypripediums, which required a high temperature for their successful cultivation, were disposed of in favour of the more easily managed cattleyas and laeleas. This move was indicative of the continuing financial problems experienced by the Society in the 1930s, which dictated that the work connected with laying out the entertainment suite took precedence over the management of the glasshouse collection. Mrs Byng Kenrick had reported to the General Committee that the inside foreman, Cyril Horton, although possessing the necessary skills required for the management of orchids, could not spare sufficient time from his duties in connection with the entertainment suite, and the Society had insufficient funds to engage a responsible man to work under Horton. But the Society's recognition of the value of the orchid collection is apparent in the allocation of funds for a new orchid house in 1939.

In the inter-war period the collection of cacti and succulents was augmented by several gifts. In 1919 Mr J. Sharp of Westbury, Wiltshire donated ten uncommon cacti, and fifty succulents were received from Kew in 1924. In the same year the Manager of the South African Railways donated several succulents that had been exhibited at the Commonwealth Exhibition at Wembley. In 1934 W. Fisher of Bearwood presented 135 cacti. The cactus and succulent collection was displayed in the house formerly leased by the University.

It will be clear from the preceding sections that gifts of specimens either from private individuals or botanical institutions were of continuing significance in augmenting the Society's collections. Commercial firms also made regular donations. Prominent among these were local firms such as John Woolman and Sons of Shirley, well-known breeders of chrysanthemums, W.H. Simpson and Sons of Edgbaston and Messrs Gunn and Sons of Olton, and nationally prominent firms such as Messrs Webb and Sons of Exeter and Messrs Barr and Sons of London.

As well as regular donations from Kew and Glasnevin, the Society received plants and seeds from the Botanical Gardens of Cambridge, Glasgow and Oxford, the Chelsea Physic Gardens, the John Innes Horticultural Institute, and European botanical gardens including those of Nancy, Wageningen, Malta and Warsaw. In 1931 the Society received a notable gift of eighty-six packets of seeds from the Royal Botanic Gardens at Edinburgh which had been collected by Clarence Elliot in northwest America. The Society received this donation through the generosity of Mr H.R. Darrah, who had made a financial contribution to the expedition and had earlier made a donation of seeds collected by Elliot in Chile.

A number of shrubs and specimen trees raised at the Gardens from the donations were planted in a new border adjacent to the rhododendron garden.

In subsequent years Elliot sponsored a number of plant-collecting expeditions employing Edward Balls as his collector. Although the Society declined to take shares in Balls' trip to Persia in 1932, it received two large donations of seeds through the generosity of W.A. Albright of Albright and Wilson, who resided in Edgbaston and who had invested in the expedition.

In the years after 1932 there was a considerable diminution in these donations from botanic institutions, commercial firms and private collectors. This can be directly attributed to the fact that the Gardens were being run without a Curator and therefore lacked an official with a network of personal contacts in the botanical and horticultural world which was an essential element in the interchange of plant material.

Throughout the years of the First World War the Society had continued to promote horticultural exhibitions in conjunction with specialist societies, which from 1915 onwards included the National Viola Society, founded in that year. Specialist Shows were held between the wars with the addition from 1933 onwards of the Alpine Garden Society's Show.

The Society's financial problems in the 1920s, however, meant that they were unable to risk expenditure on organising their own shows, which had ceased in 1915. In 1927 the Society considered reviving the Early and Midsummer Shows, but it was decided not to go forward 'on the grounds that the financial responsibility was too great'.

Although in the inter-war period the botanical and horticultural sides of the Gardens had their devotees, it was the zoological collection which proved the major attraction to visitors. Until the opening of Dudley Zoo in 1937, the Society had the only zoological collection open to the public in the Midlands. Even after the Dudley Zoo opened, the proximity of the Edgbaston collection for the citizens of Birmingham meant that this feature of the Gardens continued to be very popular. The location of the animal cages and enclosures is shown on the plan of the Gardens of 1934.

In the 1920s the Zoological Sub-Committee was chaired by Dr Rosslyn Bruce, the Vicar of St. Augustine's, Edgbaston. Dr Bruce had been an avid

Plan of the Gardens, 1934.

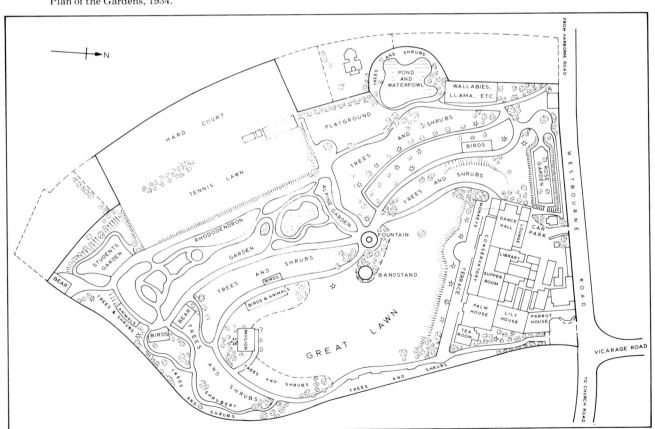

'Gladly', the first bear at the Botanical Gardens, acquired in 1921.

Edgbaston, many of whom visited the Gardens daily, accompanied by their nannies, as well as among the children from further afield, for whom a visit to see the animals was a special treat. The kids, tethered on the main lawn, had a special appeal for young children. The labels on their collars were inscribed: 'I'm Dr Bruce's kid. Whose kid are you?'

The Society also made numerous additions to the reptile collection displayed in the Lily House and to the bird collection, including an emu, a toucan, flamingoes, owls and a raven.

The collection of monkeys housed at the end of the terrace range of glasshouses always collected a large crowd of visitors. In June 1919 the Zoological Sub-Committee reported the birth of a macaque monkey, then a comparatively rare occurrence in captivity, and commented: 'The young animal has excited a great amount of interest among visitors.' A number of other baby monkeys born at the

collector of mammals, birds and reptiles from boyhood and the Society benefited considerably from his knowledge and experience.[4] He directed the activities of the Committee to increasing the mammal collection, and it acquired llamas, chimpanzees, wallabies, goats, sheep, a mongoose, a laughing jackass, a coatimundi and bears. The first bear was purchased in 1921, and named 'Gladly' by Dr Bruce – as a living embodiment of generations of childish confusion caused by the line in the well-known hymn 'Gladly my cross I'd bear'.

Gladly's death in 1927 caused widespread grief among the children, and an anonymous donor presented a Himalayan tree bear, Captain Teddy, as a replacement. In 1929 E.W. Butler donated a second bear, named Kim. All the larger animals were given names, and Rupert the ram, Walter the wallaby and Algy and Miss Issi the alligators had numerous admirers among the young residents of

'Miss Issi' the alligator, with George Cook the head animal keeper. From the *Birmingham Weekly Post*, 3 October 1931.

Interior view of the Lily House, *c.* 1934.

Gardens were successfully reared, as were several wallabies.

The introduction of another mammal proved less successful. In July 1919 a seal was purchased and placed in the basin at the base of the fountain. The first one succumbed to a throat infection, and its replacement also died, this time from swallowing a fish hook in its feed. A third seal bought in 1921 was poisoned by an outraged visitor who considered its pool too small. After that the pool was used for a collection of waterfowl.

The majority of animals were acquired by purchase, though donations from subscribers and others substantially added to the collection. In 1930, during a psittacosis scare, the Society acquired a number of parrots. A report in the *Birmingham Daily Express* of 8 July 1930 indicated that one of these acquisitions betrayed an embarrassing lack of tact. On being approached by visitors he would call out 'Hi, psittacosis' – a remark hardly calculated to increase his popularity. Nevertheless the West African parrots, who were kept in the parrot house next to the Lily House, were popular with visitors. On sunny days the parrots were placed on the terrace where they could preen their feathers and observe the antics of the 'juvenile visitors'.

Other donations came from unexpected sources. In August 1931 the Society was given an important addition to its reptile collection. On opening a box of bananas the staff of E.P. Hingley, wholesale fruit merchants, were startled to find a boa constrictor among the contents, and with some alacrity he was consigned to the Gardens.

For many years the Society was fortunate to have the services of Solomon de

Terrace scene, c. 1934.

Montford Woodward as honorary Veterinary Surgeon, who contributed much to the well-being of the collection. But the management of a zoological collection was not without its attendant problems, mainly caused by the unreliable behaviour of the general public. In May 1920 it was reported that the alligator had been blinded in one eye after being prodded by a visitor's umbrella, and the public's habit of poking their fingers through the bars of the monkeys' cage resulted in several cases of bitten fingers and torn clothing. A reporter from the *Birmingham Mail* on a visit to the Gardens in June 1930 noted the large crowd of visitors around the cages of Kim and Captain Teddy, who in spite of notices to the contrary, were being fed. In January of the following year one visitor suffered serious consequences. The early morning tranquillity of the Gardens was shattered by piercing screams from the direction of Captain Teddy's cage. When George Cook, the Head Animal Keeper, reached the scene, he found a young man inside the cage in the process of being mauled by the bear. The victim was removed to hospital, where his arm was amputated.

George Cook was Head Animal Keeper at the Gardens from 1915 to 1931, having previously worked for Sir Harvey Bruce, the cousin of Dr Rosslyn Bruce. The unfortunate incident with the bear considerably saddened the last months of his life. No reprisals were taken against Captain Teddy, who remained at the Gardens until 1937, when he was sold to Dudley Zoo.

By January 1939 the zoological collection had grown to a considerable size and at that date consisted of 80 animals, 292 birds and 26 reptiles.

An account of the Gardens in the inter-war period would be incomplete without

90

Wedding group, 1934, with the Palm House in the background.

some record of the widespread use made by individuals and organisations of the Botanical Gardens as a venue for a great variety of social events. These ranged from the garden fêtes organised by political parties, rallies of Oddfellows, Temperance galas, school and office sports and charitable fund-raising events, as well as the garden parties, wedding receptions, coming-of-age parties, silver and golden-wedding celebrations and dances organised by in-

dividuals. It is not least among the achievements of the Birmingham Botanical Gardens that such diverse activities, which were the twentieth-century equivalents of the entertainments organised by the public Pleasure Gardens of the eighteenth century and the People's Parks of the nineteenth century, could be accommodated within the setting of an institution that nevertheless retained a

Wedding Reception Dance in the Exhibition Hall, *c.* 1928.

Neville Chamberlain making his address at the Conservative and Unionist Association Fête at the Birmingham Botanical Gardens on 3 July 1937.

pronounced botanical and horticultural character.

Undoubtedly, the most popular event was the annual fête held in July by the Birmingham Conservative and Unionist Association which commenced in 1919 and continued throughout the 1920s and 30s. A regular attraction was the address given by Sir Austen Chamberlain, the Unionist MP for West Birmingham. On 3 July 1937 the guest speaker was Neville Chamberlain on his first public appearance in Birmingham following his appointment as Prime Minister, and a crowd of many thousands assembled on the great lawn to listen to his speech given from the bandstand.

Similar fêtes were also held by the Birmingham Liberal Association, though Dame Margaret Lloyd George, in her opening address to the two-day fête held in 1930, acknowledged that Birmingham was not the easiest place in the country for Liberals. In fact they had not had a Liberal member there for forty years, since the time when Mr Joseph Chamberlain changed and Birmingham changed with him.[5]

The Birmingham Borough Labour Party held its first fête at the Botanical Gardens in 1928. The star attraction of the fête in 1930 was Sir Oswald Mosley, who addressed the crowd together with Birmingham's six Labour MPs.

In June 1932 the Gardens were the setting for a Grand Garden Fête organised by the Birmingham Hospital Saturday Fund to raise money for a new Convalescent Hospital for Women at Weston-super-Mare.[6] The programme of events was designed to appeal to all age groups and included music by the band of the Fifth and Sixth Battalions of the Royal Warwickshire Regiment, children's games and sports, a Punch and Judy show, an amusement park, a display of country dances by the children of the Tilton Road schools, and dancing on the lawn, culminating in a firework display at 10 p.m.

Other organisations that regularly held events at the Gardens included the League

Crowds on the Great Lawn listening to Neville Chamberlain.

of Nations Union, the Birmingham Grocery Exchange, the Institute of Insurance Offices, the Independent Order of Oddfellows, the Temperance Society, the Walliker Society, the Birmingham Theatrical Union, the Birmingham Municipal Officers' Guild, the Birmingham Co-operative Society, the Alexandra Musical Society and the Limbless Ex-Service Men's Association. In addition, the Society itself continued to organise band concerts at Bank Holidays which attracted crowds from all over the Midlands.

Although the problems of running the Gardens in the First World War had been considerable, those during the Second World War were of a different order of magnitude. On the outbreak of war the Gardens had been without a Curator for seven years, and in spite of the efforts of the Gardens Sub-Committee and the staff, were not in the same flourishing state as they had been in 1914. The problem of retention and recruitment of the labour force reached catastrophic proportions. All the staff were liable to be called up, and the attraction of the higher wages and shorter hours of factories further depleted their numbers. The Gardens had therefore to be run by a staff consisting of those too young or too old for military service and female labour, though the latter were also subject to redeployment by the civilian authorities. To this was added the difficulty of coping with damage sustained by the glasshouses from aerial bombardment – a problem not experienced in the First War. The maintenance of a much larger zoological collection also added to the difficulties.

The minutes of the Gardens Sub-Committee meeting held on 6 September 1939 recorded the preparations taken to deal with the war emergency. Some of the Society's valuable collection of books and botanical periodicals were removed to the Chairman's house at Painswick for the duration. A brick-built room under the bandstand was prepared as an air-raid shelter, and an ARP post established in the

lodge, though after a month it was moved to a house near St. George's Church, on account of the proximity of so much glass. By December the work of erecting suitable black-out in the entertainment suite had been completed. The Zoological Sub-Committee decided, in the interests of the safety of the local inhabitants, to try to find a purchaser for the boa constrictor, but they met with no success and it had to be destroyed. The sleeping quarters of the two bears were reinforced in case the Gardens received a direct hit.

On 25 and 26 April 1940 the Daffodil and Alpine Society promoted a joint show at the Gardens, but no further exhibitions were held for the duration of the war.

In June 1940 it was decided to grant free admission to forces personnel, and the Gardens again became the setting for entertainments for wounded soldiers. On 24 June the Birmingham Fruiterers' Association entertained two hundred and fifty men from Hollymoor and Barnsley Hall Hospitals, and on 7 July the Alexandra Musical Society gave a garden party for one hundred men from the Warneford Hospital, Leamington: 'Most of these men had taken part in fighting in Belgium and France and the retreat to Dunkirk.'[7] In October the Gardens were used for a one-day conference by the National 'Dig for Victory' Campaign Council for the Midlands area. As in the First World War portions of the grounds were devoted to the cultivation of vegetables in borders in the Gardens, portions of the hothouses and on an allotment leased by the Society. Although the income produced by sales of vegetables was negligible, some of the crops provided a valuable addition to the food supplies of the zoological collection, and the Society benefited from the additional labour of Land Girls whom it was able to employ specifically for this work.

By autumn 1940 the Society was faced with new problems. The numbers of bookings for the entertainment suite had fallen drastically, and many events, including the annual Garden Party given by the Lord

Mayor, were cancelled at the last minute. This led to the loss of what had become an essential portion of the operating income, and the receipts from lettings in 1940 were only a third of the total received in 1939. The decision was taken to make a reduction in the wages bill by discharging the outside foreman, the carpenter and the weekend duty man. The reduced staff then consisted of one foreman, one journeyman gardener, two labourers, one animal keeper, one youth and two girls, and the work of the indoor and outdoor departments was merged. In March of the following year the animal keeper George Cottrell left to become an ARP warden, and the responsibility for the care of the zoological collection was assigned to the assistant keeper with additional help from the Gardens' staff. By September 1941 the staff was further reduced by resignations and call-ups and consisted of a foreman, a labourer, two girls and a youth. To the problems of maintaining grounds of twelve acres, a large hothouse collection and a zoological collection was added an unforeseen factor. After an initial decline following the outbreak of war the bookings for weddings, receptions, lunches and dances once again increased dramatically, and petrol restrictions had resulted in a considerable growth in the number of visitors. The severely-reduced Gardens' staff had therefore to devote an increasing portion of their time to clearing up after social functions and visitors, to the detriment of their gardening duties.

The Gardens Sub-Committee noted on 10 September 1941 that:

> the difficulty encountered in carrying out even the most esssential work will be realised. In addition numerous lettings during the summer have involved much extra work. Praise is due to the Staff, particularly the Indoor Foreman, for their loyal and whole-hearted service.

The Indoor Foreman, Cyril Horton, who had been employed in that capacity since 1931, was the only experienced gardener remaining in the Society's employ from the pre-war period. In April 1941 the Society appeared to be in danger of losing his services when he received his call-up papers. Fortunately an appeal for his retention was successful and he was granted reserve-occupation status.

In addition to the valiant efforts of the paid staff, the Society acknowledged its good fortune in obtaining the services of a voluntary worker – Winifred Crow. Mrs Crow had spent her childhood in Birmingham and had been a frequent visitor to the Gardens. After living in London she returned to Birmingham in 1941 where her husband held an official position. She first volunteered to work in the Gardens in July 1941, and continued to spent four days a week in weeding the borders and the Alpine Garden and assisting in general maintenance for the next four years. On 2 September 1942 the Gardens Sub-Committee noted that 'the self-sacrificing way in which she has worked is beyond praise'.

The Gardens Sub-Committee in June 1943 noted the difficulties of maintenance but recorded that the efforts of the staff were much appreciated:

> Every effort is being made to keep the Gardens as attractive and presentable as possible, but the acute shortage of labour makes this very difficult. The show of flowers in the greenhouses is well maintained and greatly admired by visitors. The spring flowering shrubs, the rhododendrons and azaleas also made an excellent show and have been the subject of many appreciative remarks by visitors to the Gardens who are coming in greatly increased numbers on fine days.

In the months between May and August 1943 the Gardens had a record total of 103,762 visitors.

Unfortunately, the behaviour of some of these visitors only added to the war-time problems 'for in spite of paper restriction the crowds are still able to indulge in their favourite pastime of throwing litter all over the place and leaving milk bottles, empty tins and other relics of a picnic behind them.'[8] In 1942 the Society was faced with major repairs. On 4 March a large section of the boundary wall to Westbourne Road collapsed from the effect of the prolonged frost. Permission for its repair was granted and the wall was reconstructed at a cost of £140.

On the night of 27 July three 500 lb. bombs fell close to the Gardens and did considerable damage to the glasshouses, blowing out 7,500 square feet of glass. The damage was patched up temporarily by the hard-pressed staff, and an immediate application for the release of the necessary materials was made. This was successful, and by March 1943 Messrs Vane and Scholefield had repaired the damage.

Although materials could be obtained for such repairs, supplies of paint and timber for routine maintenance were unobtainable and the annual programme of repairs was abandoned for the duration of the war. The Gardens Sub-Committee noted on 9th June 1943 that at the end of the five-year period expenditure of the order of £6,000 would be necessary to restore the glasshouses to their pre-war condition.

The maintenance of the zoological collection during the war was carried out under extremely difficult circumstances, caused by acute problems in obtaining foodstuffs and the shortage of labour. The Government banned the importation of bird seed in March 1941, and by June of that year coupons were issued for the purchase of cereals which covered one tenth of the Gardens' pre-war feeding-stuff purchases. At that date the Zoological Sub-Committee report noted 'the position with regard to feeding stuffs is undoubtedly very serious'. In October notices were posted in the Gardens asking for gifts of food scraps, and there was a generous response to this request by people who donated fruit, vegetables and bread. These gifts made a valuable addition to the foodstuffs, and on a subsequent occasion the Committee observed that 'some of these donors put themselves to a lot of trouble to bring these contributions'. In November 1942 the report noted that 'the general

position remains difficult and it requires much scheming and improvisation to give the animals and birds as nearly as possible a balanced ration to maintain their health and condition'. The monkeys and bears, for whom no rice could be obtained, were fed on porridge, boiled potatoes and the scraps donated by visitors. The monkeys were also the recipients of left-over sandwiches from the numerous wedding receptions held at the Gardens, when they would examine the fillings of the sandwiches minutely, discarding those that did not take their fancy. Feeding the bird collection posed the greatest problems, as supplies of bird seed were erratic, expensive and of poor quality. By October 1942 the price of parrot seed had risen to 4s a pound as against a pre-war price of threepence. To save on hay, bran and oats, the black Welsh mountain sheep were put out to graze on the Tennis Club's courts in the summers of 1942 and 1943, and in the winter were moved to the main lawn: 'their droppings will have a very beneficial effect on the lawn, the turf of which has had much hard wear in the summer, and needs a stimulating fertiliser.'[9] But through the considerable exertions of the Manager, Mr Johnstone, in obtaining foodstuffs, and the dedication of the Animal Keeper, the collection was evidently maintained in good condition. The report for 14 October 1943 noted that 'many visitors to the Gardens during the summer have remarked on the excellent condition of the animals and birds in spite of war-time conditions.' Nor were materials available to repair the cages and enclosures. On 13 June 1942 when the Gardens were thronged with two thousand visitors, ten monkeys escaped through a hole in the roof of their cage. All but one monkey was successfully recaptured. The air raid of 27 July 1942, which badly damaged the glasshouses, also blew out the glass roof of the monkeys' sleeping quarters and the parrot house, though none of the animals was harmed.

From March 1941 until November 1944 the zoological collection, which before the war had been maintained by one full-time male keeper and a half-time male assistant, was looked after by a female animal keeper, Betty Millward. Before joining the Society she had worked at Dudley Zoo for two years. At times she was helped by part-time assistants, but the Society had great difficulty in engaging assistants, and extra help had to be given by the members of the much depleted Gardens' staff and by Mr Johnstone.

After 1940 no more stock was added to the collection by purchase, but the Society received numerous donations of birds and monkeys from people who were unable to obtain suitable foodstuffs for their pets. Some of these donations came from unexpected sources. In November 1943 an Able Seaman presented a baby Chacma baboon, clothed in a miniature sailor suit, but in spite of the efforts of the Animal Keeper, it did not survive the winter. In May 1945 an Indian Lorikeet, found flying around the workroom of Chamberlain, King and Jones, was added to the collection.

5

The Search for Identity
1946-1982

The last thirty-six years of the Gardens' 150-year existence have been, in some respects, the most difficult in its entire history. They have involved considerations of the future rôle of a Garden founded primarily for the pursuit of botanical and horticultural knowledge, on to which, however, from an early date was grafted an important secondary role as a place of recreation and popular resort. In what direction was the future of this much-loved, though at times indifferently supported, institution to lie? Long before the second half of the twentieth century the botanical gardens of other urban centres had succumbed to financial pressures and had either witnessed their former glories overlain by bricks and mortar, or had been taken over by parks departments for whom, in some cases, botanic collections were secondary to the provision of public amenities. It cannot be denied that by this period the scientific rôle of botanical gardens as centres of teaching and research lay with the University Botanic Gardens, not only those of the ancient universities, but the 'red-brick' foundations of the late nineteenth century, and with the national gardens at Kew and Edinburgh. On the other hand the question may be posed whether the Birmingham Gardens had valid claims to continue as a garden that made a contribution which distinguished them from the amenities provided by a public park.

At the time of writing, the Birmingham Botanical Gardens have found a new identity as an educational and horticultural centre, and their value as a place of amenity has been more clearly recognised. The establishment of this new identity, as did its survival in the past, owes much to the continuing efforts of the members of its Committee of Management, all acting in a voluntary capacity, and to the work of numerous volunteers, as well as to the loyalty of its professional staff. To their efforts must be added the financial and moral support given by the Calthorpe Trustees, who as ground landlords of Edgbaston have assumed a role of considerable significance throughout the history of the Gardens. In recent years public bodies such as the West Midlands Council and the City of Birmingham Council have also made grants towards the maintenance of the Gardens in recognition of the unique amenity which it offers to the citizens of the Midlands.

It will be apparent from the preceding chapter that on the cessation of hostilities in May 1945, the Birmingham Botanical Gardens had survived but were in a run down and dilapidated state. The removal of the black-out covers in June 1945 revealed something of the poor condition of the glasshouses and buildings. The Gardens Sub-Committee noted at their meeting of 6 June that 'while the lighting of the premises is much improved, and the consumption of artificial light greatly restricted, the full light also shows up the wear and tear of the last six years, and the need for renovation and redecoration throughout the buildings.' The immediate post-war years, however, were marked by a

The Terrace Glasshouses, c. 1950.

period of severe constraint when materials such as timber, glass and paint were virtually unobtainable, and little could be done until the early 1950s.

The Gardens were also in a run-down state and the plant collection was depleted. The thousands of visitors who had flocked to the Gardens during the war had taken a heavy toll of the areas of lawn and the paths. Immediate restocking of plants was hampered by Government restrictions on the importation of bulbs and shrubs from Continental suppliers, and British sources had little to offer. What was available was expensive and of poor quality. The recruitment of suitable staff also exercised the Committee. By the end of 1946 the total indoor and outdoor staff had been increased to nine men, but the Gardens Sub-Committee meeting for 6

November noted that it would be necessary to have a staff of fifteen before a complete redevelopment scheme could be undertaken. Much of the time of what was essentially a garden staff had, as in the war period, to be deployed on clearing up after social functions, and on extra duties such as acting as cloakroom attendants. The Committee, however, fully recognised that a redevelopment programme of the Gardens required the expertise of a Curator, and on the retirement of the Manager, E.R. Johnstone, in 1946, it was decided to appoint a Curator. Michael Johnstone, the son of E.R., then assumed the responsibility for managing the entertainment suite. In 1959 the running of the suite was separated from the work of administering the Gardens and a new lease was negotiated with Messrs Pattison-

Hughes who now administer the entertainment suite.

Donald Harvey was appointed as Curator in March 1947. He had received his horticultural training at the Royal Horticultural Society's Gardens at Wisley and before his appointment at Birmingham had been employed by the Warwickshire Agricultural Commission. The task of restoring the Gardens to their pre-war standards occupied the next three years, and by 1950 work had been completed on replanting the rose garden, the returfing of the lawns, the thorough overhaul of the rock garden and replanting and clearing up shrub borders and terrace beds. The long border parallel to the Pinetum, formerly a herbaceous border and devoted to vegetables during the war, was planted as a monocotyledon border.

In 1947 an important innovation was introduced when the Society instituted a training scheme for student gardeners. This scheme is recognised by the Horticultural Training Boards, and students are employed by the Society for a one- or two-year period and, in addition to receiving practical training in all branches of indoor and outdoor work, attend day release courses. Many of the Society's student gardeners have been successful in gaining places at the Pershore Institute of Horticulture.

While the problems of rejuvenating the botanical side of the Gardens were acute in the post-war period, the maintenance of the zoological collection was also continued under difficult circumstances. During the war, as we have noted, materials to mend the enclosures and cages had been unobtainable, but little could be done until supplies of wire netting became available in spring 1946, when repairs assumed top priority, being completed by June of that year. The procurement of foodstuffs

The Main Lawn, *c*. 1950.

remained a pressing problem for some years, and although the price of bird seed fell after 1945, supplies were hard to come by. Due to restrictions placed on catering establishments in 1947, the valuable supply of kitchen scraps from Messrs Pattison-Hughes was greatly reduced, though potatoes and green vegetables grown at the Gardens supplemented the foodstuffs. Restocking of the collection also posed problems, and difficulties were encountered in obtaining animals in good condition at a reasonable price. In 1947 it was decided to extend the attractions by the establishment of an aquarium in the Lily House, with vivaria for snakes and other reptiles.

In 1950 the last remaining bear in the Society's collection was disposed of, being donated to Dudley Zoo, a decision forced on the Committee by an increasing number of complaints from the general public over the smallness of its enclosure. Though these protests were well intentioned, when Kim, the Himalayan bear, was moved to Dudley it was discovered that he was completely blind, and though he had been able to cope in his familiar surroundings at the Gardens he was a liability to the Zoo authorities and had to be put down. It was decided to remodel the bottom area of the Gardens comprising the bear's pen and the adjacent area of the former students' garden, which became separate enclosures for ornamental pheasants and a new wallaby area. An extensive redevelopment of the waterfowl enclosure adjacent to the children's playground was completed in 1952. The circular pond was given a new sinuous shape, the enclosure was resown and weeping willows were planted. Although a new wire fence was put up, the depredations of rats and foxes took a heavy toll of the stock, and the urban fox must be numbered among the main vandals with whom the Gardens have to contend. In 1960 a new policy was adopted over the

View from the Pinetum to the Wildfowl Enclosure, 1968.

zoological collection. Owing to rising costs it was decided to concentrate on the bird collection and smaller mammals that would appeal to children, such as rabbits, guinea pigs and monkeys, though after 1967 the keeping of monkeys was discontinued.

We must now return to the major developments in the Gardens and to the work of rebuilding the glasshouses. In 1960 it was decided to capitalise on one of the Society's assets by the sale of a property adjoining the Gardens. Westbourne, formerly the home of Neville Chamberlain, had been acquired by the Society in 1945, and it had been intended to integrate its

grounds into the existing gardens. The house and part of the grounds were sold to Edgbaston High School for Girls who at that point were vacating their buildings in Hagley Road.

The augmentation of the Society's funds by £30,000 enabled them to go ahead with three necessary projects. The first was the building of a house for the Curator. Since 1947 accommodation had been provided in a flat at Westbourne. The new house was situated beyond the rose garden and was completed in 1961 at a cost of £4,700. A wide strip of land of the former Westbourne gardens running along the north-south boundary was made into a car park, the existing car park behind the glasshouses having long proved inadequate. A

Plan of the Birmingham Botanical Gardens, June 1983.

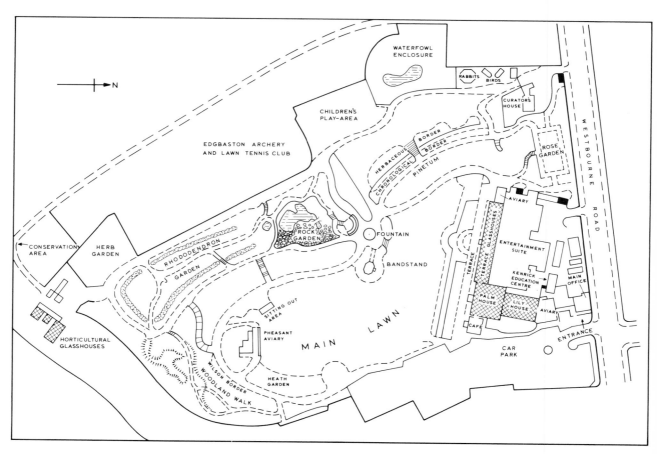

9   The Rose Garden, June 1982.   Photo: Ron Argyle & David Foster.

10　The Hugh Nettlefold Alpine Garden, 1968.　Photo: A. Gordon.

11　The Rhododendron Garden, 1968.　Photo: David Higgs.

12   The Terrace Glasshouses, June 1982.   Photo: Ron Argyle & David Foster.

13   The Lily House Pool, 1968.   Photo: Nigel Waterhouse.

14   The Fountain, June 1982, restored at the expense of the Friends of the Birmingham
Botanical Gardens to mark the sesquicentenary of the Gardens.   Photo: A. J. Ballard.

B.B.C. Gardening Club Garden.

third pressing need was for new horticultural glasshouses, and these were erected on land formerly used as allotments in the south-west area of the Gardens. At the same time an oil-fired central heating system was installed in the existing glasshouses. The remainder of the money was used on replantings in the azalea and rhododendron garden, completed in 1962.

In 1961 the Gardens were host to a new venture. The BBC decided to initiate a series of television programmes on practical gardening for the cultivators of small suburban gardens and required a demonstration plot. The Society leased to the BBC an area of ground along the southern boundary of the Gardens, in an area that had been used for the cultivation of veg-

etables during the war. The Television Gardeners' Club proved a great success, and Percy Thrower together with members of the Gardens' staff became familiar figures to many viewers of the weekly programmes. The lease was discontinued at the end of 1968, owing to a change of policy on the part of the BBC.

In 1963 work was completed on a new display area for cactus and succulents in the first terrace glasshouse. The existing collection was supplemented by plants and seeds brought back by Professor J.G. Hawkes of Birmingham University, who was a member of the General Committee, assisted by Dr Richard Lester, on a plant-collecting trip to Mexico and Central America in 1958. The plants are displayed

The Cactus Collection, June 1983.
Photo: Celia Lester.

in a naturalistic fashion with painted back-drops of desert scenery executed by John Montgomery and inspired by the layout of the Sherman Hoyt Cactus House at Kew.

During the 1960s the Committee was increasingly preoccupied by the condition of the Palm House and the other terrace glasshouses, but lack of funds precluded all but essential maintenance. But in the winter of 1967 the problem could no longer be deferred when on the night of 27 February, as a result of a gale, the roof and the walls of the Palm House parted company. An eye-witness reported that 'at one time, whole sections of the roof were going up and down like some gigantic bellows and the noise of the gale was punctuated by the crash of splintering glass'. The Committee was anxious to rebuild what was after all one of the most important features

of the Botanical Gardens. It was decided that the necessary funds would have to be raised by a special appeal, and this was launched in 1968, by the Chairman, Tony Norris. In the first months donations of £12,686 were received and reconstruction of the Palm House was begun. It was soon clear that rebuilding to the original design was out of the question, and the Palm House was rebuilt in a much simplified form but to a design that retained some of the decorative features both internally and externally.

After completion the contents were reorganised, and the Palm House is now maintained as a warm temperate house. The collection now includes two tree ferns – *Dicksonia antarctica* and the original specimen of *D.* × *lathamii* raised in the Gardens in 1872, together with cycads and palms, such as the date palm and petticoat palm (*Washingtonia*). There is also a collection of economic plants including citrus fruits, tea, coffee, cinnamon, avocado pear, eucalyptus and bamboo and a display of insectivorous plants such as Venus' fly trap, sundews and pitcher plants, together with rare ferns such as *Lygodium japonicum*. Additional colour is provided by Bougainvilleas and Strelitzias.

In 1972 the Gardens celebrated their one hundred and fortieth anniversary with a summer meeting attended by three hundred guests, including Lord Aberconway, the President of the Royal Horticultural Society.

1973 saw the renovation of another of the nineteenth-century features of the Gardens with the reconstruction of the bandstand completed in June of that year. This was celebrated in suitable style with music provided by the Third Battalion of the Royal Regiment of Fusiliers, a display of Victoriana and a concert of Victorian songs and music.

By 1974 the condition of the terrace glasshouses, erected in 1884, was giving serious cause for concern, and the western end was in imminent danger of collapse. With great generosity one of the members of the Gardens offered to replace the Western terrace glasshouse at half the cost of the lowest outside tender. An Appeal Fund was launched which was well supported, and in 1976 the glasshouse was reopened. This is now maintained as a cool temperate house with specimens grouped according to geographical areas.

In 1977 the Lily House was reconstructed to the original design, the cost being defrayed by the Calthorpe Trustees. It now houses plants representative of the world's tropical regions and includes economic plants such as banana, cotton, oil palm, sugar cane, cacao, yams, arrowroot, guava, mango, vanilla, paw-paw, cassava and loofah. The pool is planted at the margins with specimens of papyrus reed and rice, together with aquatic plants such as the sacred lotus, water hyacinth and Nile cabbage (*Pistia*). Other specimens in the Lily House include the banyan tree, orchids and exotic ferns.

The same year saw important developments in the educational potential of the Gardens with the opening of a purpose-built classroom for environmental studies. In the previous year part of the Gardens in the area formerly used by the BBC for their demonstration garden and for allotments was set up as a Conservation Area.

In 1978 the Gardens commissioned a leading landscape architect, Mary Mitchell, to prepare a plan for the long-term development of the Gardens. She recommended that they should be developed in a way that gave emphasis to historical features while at the same time incorporating new developments such as specialist areas for threatened species, both horticultural subjects and the native flora, and demonstration plots for the layout of small suburban gardens. Currently plans are in hand for the layout of a garden to be maintained by the disabled.

Recent features include a herb garden laid out in the area which was formerly the Students' Garden and then used for pheasants and wallabies. This is planted with a representative selection of over forty culinary and medicinal herbs. A chronological bed has been established near the Pinetum, and although not extensive it gives some indication of the major plant introductions over the centuries which have contributed to the immense variety of subjects cultivated in British gardens. A small shrub border has recently been established to commemorate the association of E.H. Wilson with the Gardens, and this is planted with single specimens from among his notable introductions from China in the early years of this century. It includes *Hamamelis mollis*, *Magnolia wilsonii*, *Rhododendron augustinii*, *R. sutchuenense* and *Berberis wilsoniae*. A fine specimen of one of his best known introductions – *Davidia involucrata*, the handkerchief tree – is to be found in the shrub border near the fountain.

The realisation of the educational potential of the Gardens is, in some respects, one of the most important developments in its recent history. Although the Gardens had long had a policy of allowing access to parties of school children, these visits had been of varying success, and the depredations of inadequately supervised school children had reached an unacceptable level. Anne Kenrick, for many years a member of the General Committee and Chairman of the Gardens Sub-Committee, was especially concerned with these problems. She enlisted the support of Paul Topham, an Inspector for Schools, and in 1975 the Birmingham Education Authority agreed to appoint a teacher to work at the Gardens. The first teacher, Tony Sames, started work in September 1975, and quickly established a programme of educational work. Schools that expressed an interest in using the facilities at the Gardens were visited and a programme arranged in consultation with the school, tailored to the age and ability of individual groups. Initially, teaching facilities at the Gardens were limited and children were given an introductory talk in the café before proceeding to execute worksheets and projects in the Gardens. The scheme was so well supported that the need for a permanent classroom was soon apparent. Anne Kenrick undertook the responsibility of raising the necessary funds and canvassed donations from a wide variety of sources. Major donations were received from the Stanley Smith Horticultural Trust, the Veraker Legacy, the Foyle Trust and the Friends of the Gardens, which together with other donations amounted to £17,000, and the Birmingham Education Authority defrayed the costs of equipping the classroom. The classroom was opened on 20 April 1977, the ceremony being performed by the Lord Mayor of Birmingham, Councillor Harold Powell. The Kenrick Education Centre has facilities for up to forty children and is designed to provide a flexible layout that can be used for practicals

and demonstrations, as well as for formal teaching. Although in most respects the Birmingham Botanical Gardens have perforce to operate on a scale that is far outstripped by the University and National Botanic Gardens, in the area of its educational services it can justly claim to offer a service that is unique in its scope.

Something of the special range of subjects available at the Gardens is indicated by the topics offered for study in the current programme. These include climate and vegetation; economic crops; plant physiology; plant structures and adaptations; quantitative work; trees; flower structures; herbs and spices; fresh water work; and studies of invertebrates and birds. The Gardens also provide the setting for studies in local history and urban development. In addition the Gardens continue to be a source of inspiration for art work in a variety of media including oils, water colours, embroidery and batik. Periodic displays of children's work executed as a result of their visits are mounted in the entrance corridor and are much appreciated by visitors.

A recent development in the current educational programme, initiated by the present Head of Centre, Janet Pinney, makes an important contribution to the integration of immigrant groups into the community. She has been responsible for extending educational work to nursery schools and reception centres for Asian children in the city, and parents are encouraged to accompany their children on arranged visits to the Gardens. For many of these adults the plants growing in the tropical houses are not novelties but are part of a familiar, if now distant, environment, and provide the basis for a first use of English.

As well as providing the facilities for educational visits from Local Authority schools, the Gardens have an educational programme for schools that lie outside the province of the Birmingham LEA, and for adults. This is organised by Professor Donald Skelding, formerly Professor of

The Kenrick Education Centre, June 1983. Photo: Celia Lester.

Botany at the University of the West Indies, Jamaica, and functions in much the same way as the LEA programme. The demand is such that the facilities of a second classroom are urgently required.

Professor Skelding has also been responsible, for the last three years, for a series of 'Talkabouts' organised informally for adults which take place twice a week when he conducts visitors round the hot houses and gardens.

In addition, the present Curator, Philip Butler, frequently gives talks to horti-

cultural societies, and the Head Foreman, Len Salt, has been responsible for a number of courses held at the Gardens.

A project of long-term value that the Gardens are actively engaged in concerns the Conservation Area, located beyond the part open to the general public. This was started in 1976 on the initiative of Anne Kenrick and Dr Richard Lester, chairman of the Education Sub-Committee. Its establishment was aided by two developments which were taking place at the time. The Nature Conservancy Council had recently adopted a policy of promoting urban nature reserves and gave the Society a grant of £1,500 towards the project. The necessary labour was provided under the Government's recently initiated Job Creation Scheme. The first year saw the employment of a team of eight, directed by Mark Lawley, who had first to clear away years of accumulated rubbish and to uproot portions of the allotment holders' hedges before laying paths and creating a pond. This was stocked with native species particularly those common in the Midlands area. In 1977 the Job Creation Scheme agreed to pay the wages of a second team which was directed by Professor Skelding. The original policy of allowing the vegetation to regenerate naturally was considered too slow, and a policy of plant ing native trees was adopted. These include willows, birches, aspens and poplars, some of which were obtained from the gardens of Victorian houses that were being demolished. Recent work has included the creation of an area for plants that require impeded drainage, and a dry bank area has been established for plants that need a more free-draining habitat.

Further assistance with the development of the Conservation Area was provided by the employment of two people for a one-year term under the government's Special Temporary Employment Programme, who also assisted with projects in the Gardens. They were responsible for monitoring the wild life of the Conservation Area and assisted in the continuing work of labelling specimens in the Gardens.

At present only occasional use is made of the Conservation Area in the current educational programme, but in time it will form an increasingly important adjunct to this work, providing within a small area a striking contrast of a natural environment as opposed to a man-made one.

Obtaining funds to maintain the Gardens in the second half of the twentieth century has proved no less troublesome than in preceding periods, and financial problems are necessarily a constant preoccupation for the General Committee. In 1974 the Gardens narrowly escaped closure due to the rapidly escalating cost of fuel oil and the effects of Value Added Tax introduced in that year. With great regret the Committee had to implement a doubling of members' subscriptions and a rise in entrance fees.

In the last few years, however, extra financial assistance has come from a variety of sources, not the least of which are the result of the efforts of a Friends' Group formed in 1975 under the chairmanship of Carol Hill with Sheila Langton as Secretary and Nevil Barwell as Treasurer. The fund-raising activities of this Group include a programme of lectures, an annual Christmas Fair and an annual plant sale in May. The plant sale is a most popular event and provides an opportunity for people to purchase unusual plants which are raised by Friends. To date, the Friends have donated a total of £19,000 to the Society, and as part of the celebrations marking the Gardens' sesquicentenary they defrayed the costs of restoring the fountain to working order.

In recent years the Society has also been supported in its efforts by grants from Local Authorities in recognition of the special role that the Gardens play in providing an important amenity for the citizens of Birmingham and the West Midlands. These include a grant of £20,000 from the West Midlands County Council in 1976 and a grant of £10,000 from the City of Birmingham Council in 1978, and both authorities have made further grants in subsequent years.

Recently the Society has appointed a General Manager, Leslie Godfrey, both to co-ordinate and extend its activities, in order that the Society should function on a secure financial basis.

The Society has now celebrated the one hundred and fiftieth year since the opening of its Gardens. Although the present climate of economic restrictions casts a shadow, it would not be in keeping with the spirit of the Gardens to conclude this history on a note of financial gloom. From the time of their opening in 1832, owing to the efforts of a small group of leading citizens, the Gardens have made a special contribution to the lives of millions of people resident in the Midlands. Although their primary purpose was to foster botanical and horticultural knowledge among middle-class subscribers, the opening of the Gardens to a wider public from 1844 meant that for a period of years the Gardens provided one of the few breathing spaces available to those whose lives were otherwise confined to the factory or workshop. By the end of the nineteenth century when the need for public open spaces had been met in large measure by the municipal authority and by individual philanthropists, the Gardens continued to fill a role as a place of popular resort, especially at Bank Holidays, while at the same time retaining a standard of excellence among provincial botanical gardens. The fusion of its two roles has been no less evident in the twentieth century. While the scientific aspects have at times been under pressure, because the Society had to concentrate on more popular features in order to obtain sufficient funds for survival, the maintenance of a zoological collection and the provision of a spectacular setting for both private entertaining and insti-

tutional fund-raising events must not be regarded as mere expedients, but as part of a many-faceted contribution made by the Gardens to the enrichment of the lives of countless individuals.

In the last few years the Gardens have assumed a leading position in the environmental education of school children, and it is to be hoped that sufficient funds will be forthcoming to allow the Society to extend this work to visitors of all age groups. The Gardens of the BBHS are a superb amenity that has a wide application.

It is perhaps fitting to close this history with an excerpt from a letter received as a result of an appeal for recollections of the Gardens, which serves to indicate that the efforts of a few have contributed greatly to the happiness of many:

Does the memory of happiness count? Some of my first memories are of being taken to the Gardens in my 'best', by my Aunt in the early twenties. It was a wonderland for a small child; tall trees, all those flowers; the strange almost strangling smell of the hothouse and of course the animals; to this day I can remember the potent smell of the foxes and the monkeys, who according to my Aunt 'were rude' and I was always dragged off! When I had my own children, going to the Gardens was one of our treats; and having tea and cakes at the Tea Room was very special. My only sadness is that all my grandchildren live so many thousands of miles away, so going to the Gardens is a talked-about and not actually experienced pleasure for them.

Notes

Introduction (pp. 11-13)

[1] Three botanic gardens founded in Ireland were associated with universities. These were the Trinity College Botanic Gardens at Ballsbridge, opened in 1806, and the Botanic Gardens of Cork and Galway University Colleges opened in the mid-nineteenth century. In addition the Royal Cork Institution maintained a botanic garden between 1809 and 1829 (Eileen McCracken, *The Palm House and Botanic Garden, Belfast*, Ulster, 1971, p. 8).

[2] The Botanic Gardens of the Royal Caledonian Society in Edinburgh received an annual government grant of £200 from 1853 until 1858. In 1864 they were amalgamated with the Royal Botanic Garden of Edinburgh (H.R. Fletcher and W.H. Brown, *The Royal Botanic Garden, Edinburgh 1670-1970*, Edinburgh, 1970, pp. 147-8). The Gardens run by the Royal Botanic Institution of Glasgow received a substantial donation from the University in order that its students might attend lectures there. The Physic Garden of the Old College, established in 1705, had not been maintained after *c.* 1805 (E.W. Curtis, *Glasgow Botanic Gardens*, Glasgow, 2nd edition 1979, p. 2).

[3] Kenneth Lemmon, 'The hunt for new plants' in John Harris (ed.), *The Garden: A Celebration of One Thousand Years of British Gardening*, 1979, p. 96.

[4] I am indebted to Kenneth Lemmon for this information.

[5] David Cannadine, *Lords and Landlords: The Aristocracy and The Towns, 1774-1967*, Leicester, 1980, p. 98.

[6] Cannadine, op. cit., p. 157.

Chapter 1: A Promising Beginning, 1829-1845 (pp. 15-35)

[1] *Aris's Gazette*, 28 September 1829, quoted in Robert Dent, *Old and New Birmingham* (first published Birmingham, 1878-1880, reprinted Wakefield, 1973) Vol. II, p. 422.

[2] BBHS Manuscript Collection BG 2/1/1, Minutes of the General Committee, 19 October 1830.

[3] BG 2/1/1 Minutes of the General Committee, 15 December 1830.

[4] BG 33/1/5 J.C. Loudon to Thomas Knott, 21 February 1831.

[5] The Gardens Sub-Committee Minutes for 12 April 1842 (BG 2/3/1/2) include a letter from Cameron in which he states that at the commencement of the Gardens he disclaimed any pretensions as a landscape gardener.

[6] John Gloag, *Mr Loudon's England*, London, 1970, p. 63.

[7] Loudon was subsequently responsible for the layout of a less exclusive botanic garden when he prepared the plans of the Derby Arboretum, the gift of Joseph Strutt to that town in 1840.

[8] Vol. VII, 1831, pp. 399-415; Vol. VIII, 1832, pp. 110-12.

[9] BG. 2/1/1/1 Minutes of the General Committee, 10 May 1831.

[10] BG 43/1 Rees Davies to William Sands Cox, 26 June 1829.

[11] BG 33/6/1 John Shepherd to J.W. Crompton 25 January 1831.

[12] 'Description of a design made for the Birmingham Horticultural Society, for laying out a Botanical Horticultural Garden, adapted to a particular situation' in *The Gardener's Magazine*, Vol. VIII, 1832, pp. 407-28.

[13] BG 2/3/1/1 Gardens Sub-Committee Minute Book, 30 May 1831.

[14] Roy Anderson, *From Greenhouse to Conservatory* (unpublished dissertation, Birmingham School of Architecture, 1968), p. 39. In 1835 the firm were responsible for a metallic Conservatory for the Manchester Botanical and Horticultural Society, ibid., p. 70.

[15] *The Gardener's Magazine*, Vol. VIII, 1832, p. 428.

[16] Two writers have advanced the opinion that little, if anything, of Loudon's plans for the Birmingham Botanical Gardens was in fact executed. See Miles Hadfield, 'Garden design ahead of its time', *Country Life*, Vol. 147, 7 May 1970, p. 1071, and John Hix, *The Glass House*, London, 1974, p. 111. They have been misled by two factors – the rejection of his circular arrangement of the glasshouses and the fact that the area of the Gardens was substantially reduced in 1844.

[17] *The Gardener's Magazine*, Vol. VIII, 1832, p. 427.

[18] BG 37/1/1 John Lindley to Dr John Darwall, Chiswick, 22 August 1831.

[19] This section is based on a list, in Cameron's handwriting, of contributors of plants and seeds (BG 37/1/3). It is undated, but it can be inferred that it was drawn up in 1833, as the Society has a collection of sixteen transport labels that accompanied the plants in 1833 and these accord with the donors in Cameron's list (BG 45/1-16).

[20] *Glasgow Herald*, 13 April 1894. I am indebted to the Principal Archivist, Strathclyde Regional Archives, for this reference.

[21] George F. Chadwick, *The Park and the Town*, London, 1966, p. 149.

[22] BG 37/1/3.

[23] Sir William Hooker resided at West Park until he moved to Methold House, which was henceforth to become the official residence of the Director in 1852 (Wilfred Blunt, *In for a Penny: A Prospect of Kew Gardens*, London, 1978, p. 87, p. 93).

[24] BG 2/3/1/2 Gardens Sub-Committee Minutes, 19 January 1841; 16 March 1841.

[25] Ibid., 21 May 1841; 21 December 1841.

[26] BG 2/1/1/1 Minutes of the General Committee, Mr Knowles' report to A.G.M. 15 October 1834.

[27] For the subsequent fate of this collection see p.47.

[28] *The Gardeners' Chronicle*, 24 August, 1844, pp. 574-5.

[29] BG 43/3 William Withering to Thomas Lee, 15 August 1829.

[30] BG 43/5 John Sabine to John Linwood, 23 February 1830.

[31] Quoted in Robert Langford, *A Century of Birmingham Life*, Birmingham, 1875, pp. 562-3.

[32] BG 3/2 Exhibition Committee Minutes, Plan of the Exhibitions, 3 June 1833.

[33] BG 2/1/1/1 Minutes of the General Committee, Mr Knowles' report to AGM, 11 September 1833.

[34] BG 3/2 Exhibition Committee Minutes, 11 June 1834.

[35] BG 2/1/1/1 Minutes of the General Committee, Mr Knowles' report to the AGM, 16 October 1834.

[36] BG 2/1/1/1 Minutes of the General Committee, AGM, 24 September 1835.

[37] The costs of the glasshouses, lodge and boundary wall amounted to £3,650, and £1,400 had been spent on acquiring the lease, surveyors' and solicitors' fees, plans and plants, of which sum £967 had been spent on taking over Mr Aspley's lease of his house and its immediate grounds.

[38] *Glasgow Herald*, 13 April 1894.

[39] Chadwick, op. cit., p. 96.

[40] A.L. Winning, *A Short History of the Sheffield Botanic Gardens*, p. 7. *Leeds Intelligencer*, 4 July 1840.

[41] Eileen McCracken, *The Palm House and Botanic Garden, Belfast*, Ulster 1971, p. 14.

Chapter 2: The 'Ornamental' versus the 'Scientific', 1846-1883 (pp. 37-57)

[1] BG 2/1/1/2 Minutes of the General Committee, 24 March 1846.

[2] Ibid., 31 March 1846..

[3] *Midland Counties Herald* 26 September 1846.

[4] Annual Report 1846.

[5] Annual Report 1847.

[6] Annual Report 1849. It would appear that during Cameron's curatorship the plant tallies had consisted of a number and part of the name, and reference had to be made to a full list kept by him.

[7] Quoted in Blunt, op. cit., p. 107.

[8] Ibid. p. 108.

[9] BG 2/3/1/2 Gardens Sub-Committee Minute Book, 26 August 1861.

[10] Berrow Court appears on the far left of Elizabeth Phipson's painting of the Gardens (Plate 8).

[11] BG 2/1/1/4 Gardens Sub-Committee Minutes, 4 May 1865.

[12] 18 November 1865, p. 1087.

[13] Birmingham University Library, Chamberlain Collection, AC/1/1/2, Journal of Caroline Kenrick.

[14] *The Illustrated London News*, 21 June 1851. p. 585.

[15] This section is based on an autobiographical account of Latham's career published in *The Gardeners' Chronicle*, 25 July 1903, p. 53.

[16] Ibid.

[17] Twenty years previously this firm had supplied the glass for the Crystal Palace.

[18] Between 1851 and 1868 Frederick, Lord Calthorpe, had continued the policy adopted by his brother George of foregoing the ground rent on the house, charging the Society a reduced rent. From 1868, Frederick Henry, Lord Calthorpe, continued the liberality of the family in that although the Society were henceforth to pay the total rent, this was offset by an annual donation of £100.

[19] Annual Report, 1874.

[20] These articles appeared in the issues of 22 June, 28 September, and 12 October, 1872; 13 June, 1874; 9 January, 1875; 16 June, 1877; 13 September, 1879; 20 August, 1881; 14 July and 21 July, 1883.

[22] In 1889 the stock of *Cypripedium* × *lathamianum* was sold to Veitch and Sons for £225.

Chapter 3: Developments and Diversification, 1884-1913 (pp. 59-80)

[1] BG 2/1/1/5 General Committee Minutes, Report of the Buildings Sub-Committee, 2 January 1884.

[2] [Walter Chamberlain], *Birmingham Botanical and Horticultural Society, a brief summary of its history; its objects and utility; its finances; and its present position*, Birmingham, 1885, p. 9.

[3] BG 24/7/35 M.R. Avery to Hugh Nettlefold, 28 April 1884.

[4] BG 24/7/8 Lord Dartmouth to P.D. Bennett, 15 February 1884.

[5] BG 24/7/18 R.S. Hudson to H. Nettlefold, 27 February 1884.

[6] Donations to the New Building Fund, Annual Report 1884.

[7] The total costs amounted to just under £3,000, which included the glass and the heating arrangements. As for the Palm House, the glass was supplied at cost price by the firm of Chance Brothers.

[8] Annual Report 1895.

[9] Annual Report 1895.

[10] E.W. Curtis, *A Guide to The Glasgow Botanic Gardens*, Glasgow, second edition 1979, pp. 2-3.

[11] McCracken, op. cit., p. 27, p. 54.

[12] A.L. Winning, *A Short History of the Sheffield Botanic Gardens*, Sheffield, 1970, p. 7.

[13] *The Gardeners' Chronicle*, 18 September 1875; 31 July 1880; 31 March 1883. I am grateful to the City Archivist of Kingston-upon-Hull for additional information in this paragraph.

[14] Annual Report for 1902-3.

[15] These appeared in the issues of February 1891; 26 November 1892; 6 May, 10 June and 9 December 1893; 10 August 1895; 19 September 1896; 2 May 1903; 7 May 1904; 5 May 1906; 17 December 1910.

[16] R.A. Rolfe, *Handlist of Orchids cultivated in the Royal Gardens*, London, 1896.

[17] 'Birmingham half-holiday resorts', *Birmingham Faces and Places*, Vol. I, 1888-9, p. 53.

[18] Annual Report, 1900-1901.

[19] Annual Report, 1891-1892.

Chapter 4: The Gardens in War and Peace, 1914-1945 (pp.81-97)

[1] Memorandum and Articles of Association of the BBHS, 18 June 1930.

[2] Phyllis Rodway and Lois Slingsby, *Philip Rodway and a Tale of Two Theatres*, Birmingham, 1934, p. 223.

[3] Annual Report, 1925.

[4] Verily Anderson, *The Last of the Eccentrics: A Life of Rosslyn Bruce*, London, 1972, pp. 217-18.

[5] *Birmingham Post*, 30 June 1930.

[6] The fund had first been organised in Birmingham in 1869 and was an extension of the Birmingham Hospital Sunday Fund pioneered in Birmingham in 1859 and widely imitated throughout the country. The Hospital Saturday Fund initially raised contributions in workshops and manufactories for the support of the voluntary-aided hospitals and convalescent homes. It continues in operation to the present day.

[7] BG 2/3/2/8 Gardens Sub-Committee Reports, 10 July 1940.

[8] BG 2/3/2/8, Gardens Sub-Committee Reports, 7 July 1943.

[9] BG 2/4/2/1 Zoological Sub-Committee Reports, 11 November 1943.

Bibliography

Birmingham Botanical and Horticultural Society

General Committee Minutes, 1829-1969
Gardens Sub-Committee Minutes, 1831-1886; 1902-1963
Gardens Sub-Committee Reports, 1902-1966
Zoological Sub-Committee Minutes, 1919-1963
Exhibition Committee Minutes, 1833-1843
United Exhibition Committee Minutes, 1836
Education Sub-Committee Minutes, 1975-1981
Correspondence relating to appointment of Curator, 1831
Correspondence concerning the New Buildings Fund, 1884
General Correspondence
List of Plants and Seeds sent by L.H.S. to B.B.H.S., August 1831
List of Contributors of plants by B.B.H.S. and names of those to whom plants distributed (no date)
Memorandum and Articles of Association of the B.B.H.S., 1930
Annual Reports: 1841-1847; 1849-1859; 1861-1866; 1868; 1871-1915; 1932; 1936-1937; 1953; 1958-1978
Press Cuttings Albums: 1900, 1901-1902, 1903-1905, 1930-32

Birmingham Reference Library

Plan of Mr Aspley's land at Edgbaston (B.R.L. 383101)
Birmingham Horticultural Society Leaflets, Newspaper Cuttings, Reports, etc. (B.R.L. 520443)

Birmingham University Library

Chamberlain Collection, The Journals of Caroline Kenrick AC 1/1/2

Dissertation

Anderson, Roy, *From Greenhouse to Conservatory* (unpublished dissertation, Birmingham School of Architecture, 1968)

Periodical Literature

Aris's Gazette
Midland Counties Herald
Birmingham Faces and Places
The Gardeners' Chronicle
The Gardener's Magazine
The Gardeners' Magazine

Printed Literature

Anderson, Verily, *The Last of the Eccentrics: a life of Rosslyn Bruce*, London 1972
Blunt, Wilfred, *In For a Penny: a prospect of Kew Gardens*, London 1978
Cannadine, David, *Lords and Landlords: the aristocracy and the towns, 1774-1967*, Leicester 1980
Chadwick, G.F., *The Park and The Town: public landscape in the nineteenth and twentieth centuries*, London 1966
[Chamberlain, Walter], *The Birmingham Botanical and Horticultural Society. A Brief Summary of its History; its Objects and Utility; its Finances; and its present position; together with some account of The New Glass Houses, and a Moral*, Birmingham 1885
Curtis, E.W., *Glasgow Botanic Gardens*, Glasgow, 2nd edition 1979
Dent, Robert, *Old and New Birmingham*, vol. III, Birmingham 1878-1880, reprinted Wakefield 1973
Gloag, John, *Mr Loudon's England*, London 1970
Hillhouse, W. and Latham, W.B., *Catalogue of*

the Collections, ii. List of Ferns and Fern Allies*, Birmingham 1894

Hix, John, *The Glass House*, Oxford 1974

Knowles, G.M. and Westcott, Frederic, *The Birmingham Botanic or Midland Floral Magazine*, London 1836

Knowles, G.M. and Westcott, Frederic, *The Floral Cabinet or Magazine of Exotic Botany*, London 1837-1839

[Knowles, G.M. and Westcott, Frederic], *Catalogue of the Plants Cultivated in The Birmingham Botanic Garden* Part One: Trees and Shrubs, Birmingham [1836]

Langford, J.A., *A Century of Birmingham Life*, Birmingham 1868

Lemmon, Kenneth, 'The hunt for new plants' in John Harris (ed.), *The Garden: A celebration of one thousand years of British gardening*, 1979

Maund, Benjamin, *The Botanist*, London 1837-1842

McCracken, Eileen, *The Palm House and Botanic Garden, Belfast*, Ulster 1971

Rodway, Phyllis and Slingsby, Lois, *Philip Rodway and a Tale of Two Theatres*, Birmingham 1934

Rolfe, R.A., *Hand-List of Orchids Cultivated in the Royal Gardens*, London 1896

Saunders, Ann, *Regent's Park*, Newton Abbot 1969

Winning, A.L., *The Sheffield Botanical Gardens*, Sheffield 1970

Appendix

*Presidents of the Birmingham Botanical
and Horticultural Society*

1829-1853	William, 4th Earl of Dartmouth
Dec. 1853-1868	Frederick, 4th Lord Calthorpe
June 1868-1893	Frederick Henry, 5th Lord Calthorpe
Oct. 1893-1910	Augustus Cholmondely, 6th Lord Calthorpe
Dec. 1910-1957	Fitzroy Hamilton Anstruther-Gough-Calthorpe
April 1957-	Brigadier Sir Richard Anstruther-Gough-Calthorpe

Chairmen of the General Committee

Before 1846 the Chairmanship of the General Committee changed from meeting to meeting, the chairman being elected by the attendance of the day. From 1846 until 1886 the chairman was elected by the Committee to serve for one year. In 1886 the rules were officially changed to allow for re-election in subsequent years.

1847	W. Room	1864	C.L. Browning
1848	W. Elliott	1865	Edwin Yates
1848	Charles Edge	1866	H. Christian
1850-51	Thomas Osborn	1867	R.H. Milward
1852	J.A. Campbell	1868	Edwin Yates
1853	W.R. Kettle	1869	J.T. Collins
1854	Edmund Heeley	1870	George Dixon
1855	John Ratcliff	1871	Frederick Rayner
1856	C.W. Elkington	1872	Samuel Worsey
1857	John Manley	1873	Thomas Osborn
1858	H. Christian	1874	J.W. Ingram
1859	J.A. Campbell	1875	Thomas Osborn
1860	W. Bolton	1876	J. Walford
1861	Edwin Yates	1877	P.D. Bennett
1862	H. Christian	1878	Ashley Bolton
1863	J.T. Collins	1879	J. Morley

1880-81	William Southall	1944	H. Burman
1882-84	P.D. Bennett	1945-46	T.J. Score
1885-87	Walter Chamberlain	1947-52	L. Arthur Smith
1888-91	Leonard Brierley	1953-60	Charles Beale
1892-93	Henry Buckley	1961-69	C.A. Norris
1894-99	Edward Bliss	1970-71	E.R. Payne
1900-01	J.O. Mayne	1972-74	G.F. Egan
1902-03	J.H. Poynting	1975-76	B.G. Dibble
1904-08	William Hillhouse	1977-78	B.J. Clatworthy
1909-10	J.H. Poynting	1979-80	Harold Royle
1911-24	W.H. Whitlock	1981-	Michael Worley
1925-43	W.I. Good		

Curators

April 1831-June 1847	David Cameron
July 1847-Nov. 1867	C.H. Catling
Jan. 1868-Sept. 1903	William Bradbury Latham
Oct. 1903-Oct. 1932	Thomas Humphreys
May 1947-July 1959	Donald Harvey
Dec. 1960-Apr. 1964	Geoffrey Collins
May 1964-Apr. 1969	John Warrington
May 1969-	Philip Butler

CATALOGUE

OF

PLANTS

CULTIVATED IN THE

BIRMINGHAM BOTANIC GARDEN,

ARRANGED ACCORDING TO THE

NATURAL AND LINNÆAN SYSTEM;

TOGETHER WITH THEIR

SYSTEMATIC AND ENGLISH NAME,

NATIVE COUNTRY,

TIME OF INTRODUCTION, THE SOIL IN WHICH THEY THRIVE BEST,
AND WHERE FIGURED.

ALSO, A

COPIOUS LIST OF SYNONYMES,

COLLATED FROM THE BEST AUTHORITIES.

———

BIRMINGHAM:

PUBLISHED BY JOHN M. KNOTT, BOOKSELLER,

95, HIGH-STREET.

———

PRINTED BY THOMAS KNOTT, HIGH-STREET.

PART I.

TREES AND SHRUBS.

The Compiler, in sending the following Catalogue to press, has to acknowledge that he has received much assistance from the *Hortus Britannicus*, by Mr. Loudon.

In the Natural Arrangement he has followed the *Prodromus Systematis Naturalis Regni Vegetabilis*, by Professor De Candolle.

The Synonymes, which are printed in Italics, have been obtained from Professor De Candolle's work above quoted, and the *Nomenclator Botanicus* by Dr. Steudel, and from such other works of authority as the Compiler had access to.

On the completion of the Parts, the whole of the Abbreviations will be explained in an Appendix.

ERRATA.

Page 6, line 5 from the top, place Sect. 1. after Evonymus, instead of after Europæus.
Page 16, line 2 from the top, *for* Cratægus *read* Amelanchier.

| NATURAL SYSTEM. | | | | LINNEAN SYSTEM. | | |

Order, RANUNCULACEÆ. Juss.   Class, POLYANDRIA. Order, POLYGYNIA.

Tribe I. *Clematideæ.* De Cand. Syst. Vol. i. p. 131.

No.	Systematic Name.	Authority.	English Name.	Native Country.	Time of Introd.	Soil.	Where figured.
	CLEMATIS	Lin.	Virgin's bower				
	(Sect. 1. *Flowers in panicles, leaves pinnate, or bipinnate.*)						
1	flammula	Lin.	flame	South of France	1597	com. gard.	Knor. Thes. 2. 9.
2	orientalis	Lin.	oriental	Levant	1731	......	Dil. Elth. 119—145
	flava. Moench.						
3	glauca	Willd.	glaucous	Siberia	1731	......	Wat. Den. Br. 73
4	vitalba	Lin.	white vine	England		......	Eng. Bot. 612
	(Sect. 2. *Flowers in panicles, leaves ternate, or biternate.*)						
5	Virginiana	Lin.	Virginian	N. America	1767	sand and peat	Wat. Den. Br. 74
6	triternata	De Cand.	triternate	unknown	1800	peat and loam	
	Atragene triternata. Desfont.						
	(Sect. 3. *Flowers solitary, one flowered, leaves pinnate, rarely ternate.*)						
7	Viorna	Lin.	Traveller's joy	Carolina	1732	com. gard.	Dil. Elth. 118—144
8	augustifolia	Jacq.	narrow lvd.	Dahuria	1787	peat and loam	Wat. Den. Br. 112
	lasiantha. Fisch. *Pallasii.* Gmel.						
	(Sect. 4. *Peduncles solitary, one flowered, leaves undivided.*)						
9	florida	Thunb.	florid	Japan	1776	sand and loam	Bot. Mag. 834
10	flor. pleno.		double flowered		1569	......	
	Atragene indica. Desfont.						
11	viticella	Lin.	Vine bowered	N. Europe	1810	com. gard.	Bot. Mag. 565
	lugubris. Salisb. *Viticella deltoidea.* Moench.						
12	campaniflora	Brot.	bell flowered	Lusitania	1810	sand and loam	Bot. Cab. 867
13	crispa	Lin.	curled flowered	N. America	1826	peat and loam	Bot. Mag. 1892
14	cirrhosa	Lin.	tendrilled	Spain	1596	com. gard.	Flor. Græc. 51
	Atragene cirrhosa. Pers.						
15	Balearica	Rich.	Balearic	Minorca	1783	......	Bot. Mag. 259
	calycina. Ait. *Atragene balearica.* Pers.						
16	alpina	Mill.	alpine	Europe	1792	......	Bot. Repos. 180
	Atragene Austriaca. B. M. *Alpina.* L.						
17	macropetala	Ledeb.	long petaled	Altai Mts.	1827	peat and sand	Led. Ic. Fl. Ross. t. 11
	Atragene macropetala. Meyer.						
18	Sibirica	Mill.	Siberian	Siberia	1753	peat and sand	Pall. Ross. 2 76
19	Lathyrifolia	Bess.	Lathyrus lvd.		1834	peat and loam	

Tribe V. *Pæoniaceæ.* De Cand.

	ZANTHORHIZA	Marsh	Yellow root		Class, PENTANDRIA. Order, POLYGYNIA. Lin.		
20	apiifolia	L'her	parsley leaved	N. America	1796	com. gard.	
	PÆONIA	Lin.	Pæony		Class, POLYANDRIA. Order, DIGYNIA.		
21	moutan	Sims	Chinese tree	China	1789	peat and loam	Bot. Mag. 1154
22	1 papaveracea	Bot. Repos.	poppy flowered			......	Bot. Repos. 463
23	2 Banksii	Bot. Repos.	Bank's			......	Bot. Repos. 448
24	3 rosea	Bot. Repos.	rose flowered			......	Bot. Repos. 373

Order, MAGNOLIACEÆ. De Cand. theor. 213.   Class, POLYANDRIA. Order, POLYGYNIA. Lin.

Tribe II. *Magnolieæ.* De Cand.

	MAGNOLIA	Lin.					
	(Sect. 1. *Species American, ovaria approximating, anthers turning from their axis.*)						
25	grandiflora	Lin.	large flowered	N. America	1734	loam and peat	
26	1 exoniensis		Exeter	......		......	Bot. Cab. 814
27	2 ferruginea		rusty	......		......	Bot. Mag. 1952
28	3 obtusifolia		obtuse leaved	......		......	
29	4 oblongifolia		oblong leaved	......		......	
30	glauca	Lin.	glaucous	......	1688	......	Bot. Mag. 2164
	fragrans	Salisb.	fragrant				
31	1 arborea				1817	......	
32	4 Thomsoniana	Hortul.	Thomsons			......	
33	acuminata	Lin.	acuminated	N. America	1736	sand and loam	Bot. Cab. 419
	Eustica	Hortul.		......		......	
	pensylvanica	Hortul.	Pensylvanian	......			
34	auriculata	Lam.	ear leaved		1786	peat and loam	Bot. Mag. 1206
	auricularis	Salisb.		......		......	
	Fraseri	Walt.	Frasers	......			
35	macrophylla	Michx.	long leaved	......	1800	......	Bot. Mag. 1189
	Michauxia	Hortul.	Michaux's	......			
36	cordata	Michx.	heart leaved		1801	sand and loam	Bot. Cab. 474
37	maxima	Lod.	largest		1820	peat and loam	
38	pyramidata	Bart.	pyramidal		1811	......	Bot. Reg. 407
39	umbrella	Lam.	shady		1752	sand and loam	Michx. arb. 5
	tripetala		three petaled				
	(Sect. 2. *Species Asiatic, ovaria somewhat distant, anthers turning to their axis.*)						
40	Yulan	Desf.		China	1789	peat and loam	Bot. Mag. 1621
	conspicua	Salisb.	conspicuous	......	1789	......	
	Precia	Correa.		......	1789	......	

A

No.	Systematic Name.	Authority.	English Name.	Native Country.	Time of Introd.	Soil.	Where figured.
	MAGNOLIA.						
41	obovata	Thunb.	obovate	Japan		loam and peat	
42	Soulangiana	Hort.	Soulanges	Hybrid	1826	peat and loam	
	LIRIODENDRON	Lin.	Tulip tree				
43	tulipifera	Lin.	Tulip bearing	N. America	1663	sand and loam	Bot. Mag. 275

Order, ANONACEÆ. Juss. Gen. 283. De Cand. Sys. i. p. 463.   Class, POLYANDRIA. Order, POLYGYNIA.

	ASIMINA	Adans					
44	triloba	Dunal	three lobed	N. America	1736	peat and loam	Cat. Car. 283
	Anona triloba	Lin.					
	ANONA	Adans					
45	glabra	Lin.	Custard apple smooth fruited	Carolina	1774	rich mould	Cat. Car. 2 64

Order, MENISPERMACEÆ. Juss. Gen. 284.   Class, DIŒCIA. Order, DODECANDRIA. Lin.

Tribe II. *Menispermeæ.*

	MENISPERMUM Tourn.						
46	Canadense	Lin.	Canadian	N. America	1691	sand and peat	Bot. Mag. 1910
47	Dauricum	De Cand.	Daurian	Dahuria	1810	......	Deless. 1, 100
	COCCULUS	C. Bauh.					
48	Carolinus	De Cand.	Carolina	N. America	1759	com. gard.	
	Wendlandia populifolia.	Willd.					

Order, BERBERIDEÆ. Vent. tabl. 3, p. 13.   Class, HEXANDRIA. Order, MONOGYNIA. Lin.

| | BERBERIS | Lin. | Berberry | | | | |

(Sect. 1. *Leaves simple, peduncles many flowered, racemose.*)

49	Vulgaris	Lin.	common	Europe		com. gard.	Eng. Bot. 49
50	1 fructu alba		white fruited			......	
51	2 fructu lutea		yellow fruited			......	
52	Canadensis	Mill.	Canadian	N. America	1759	......	
53	Sinensis	Desf.	Chinese	China	1815	......	Wat. Den. Br. 26

(Sect. 2. *Leaves simple, pedicels one flowered.*)

54	empetrifolia	Lam.	empetrum leaved.	Magellan		loam and peat	
55	heterophylla	Juss.	various leaved	......	1805	com. gard.	Hook Fl. Ex. 14
56	Sibirica	Pall.	Siberian	Siberia	1790		Bot. Reg. 487
57	rotundifolia		round leaved				
58	dulcis	Swt.	sweet fruited	Magellan	1830	......	Swt. Fl. Gar. 2 s. 100
	MAHONIA	Nutt.					
59	fascicularia	De Cand.	bundled	California	1819	......	Bot. Mag. 2396
	Berberis pinnata	Lag. }	pinnate	......			
	fasciculata	Sims. }					
60	glumacea	De Cand.	glumaceous	America		loam and peat	
	repens	G. Don.	creeping	N. America	1824	......	

Order, CRUCIFERÆ. Juss Gen. 237. De Cand. Sys. 2. p. 139.   Class, TETRADYNAMIA. Lin.

Sub-Order 1st. PLEURORHIZEÆ. De Cand. Sys. 2. p. 146.

Tribe I. *Arabideæ seu Pleurorhizeæ Siliquosæ.* De Cand. Sys. 2. p. 146.

	CHEIRANTHUS	Brown	Wall flower				
61	cheiri	Lin.	garden			com. gard.	
62	fruticulosus	Lin.	shrubby			......	

Tribe III. *Thlaspideæ seu Pleurorhizeæ Angustiseptæ.* De Cand. 2 p. 373.

	IBERIS	Lin.	Candy tuft				
63	sempervirens	Lin.	evergreen	Candia	1731	......	Riv tetr. 224, 2
64	saxatilis	Lin.	rock	S. Europe	1739	......	Gar. Aix 101
65	2 corifolia	B. M.	coris leaved	......	1800	......	Bot. Mag. 1642

Tribe IX. *Lepidineæ seu Notorhizeæ Angustiseptæ.* De Cand. 2. p. 521.

| | ÆTHIONEMA | Brown | | | | | |
| 66 | membranaceum | De Cand. | memb. podded | Persia | | ...... | Swt. Fl. Gar. 2 s. t. 69 |

Tribe XIII. *Velleæ seu Orthoploceæ Latiseptæ.* De Cand. 2. p. 639.

| | VELLA | De Cand | | | | | |
| 67 | pseudocytisus | Lin. | bastard cytisus | Spain | 1759 | com. gard. | Cav. icon. 1, 42 |

Order, CISTINEÆ. De Cand. Prod. 1. p. 263.   Class, POLYANDRIA. Order, MONOGYNIA. Lin.

| | CISTUS | Tourn. | Rock rose | | | | |

(Sect. 1. *Petals rose, red, or purple coloured.*)

68	purpureus	Lam.	purple			peat and loam	Swt. Cist. 17
	Alabastrum magnum }	Ker.	large			......	
69	parvifolius	Lam.				......	
70	villosus	Lam.	villous	S. Europe	1640	......	Duham Arb. 1, 64
71	vaginatus	Ait.	sheathed	Teneriffe	1779	......	Swt. Cist. 9
	pilosus	Lin.	hairy				....
72	rotundifolius	Swt.	round leaved	S. Europe		sand and loam	Swt. Cist. 75
	villosus 2 *virescens* }	De Cand.					

(Sect. 2. *Petals white, or whitish.*)

| 73 | salvifolius | Lin. | sage leaved | S. Europe | 1548 | sand and peat | Swt. Cist. 54 |
| | *femina* | Clus. | female | ...... | | ...... | .... |

No.	Systematic Name.	Authority.	English Name.	Native Country.	Time of Introd.	Soil.	Where figured.
	CISTUS.						
74	cobariensis	Pourr.	cobor	Spain	1656	sand and peat	Swt. Cist. 8
	hybridus	Pourr.	hybrid	......		......	....
75	Monspeliensis	Lin.	Montpelier	S. Europe	1656	......	Jacq. Col. 2, 8
76	hirsutus	Lam.	hairy	Portugal	1656	......	Swt. Cist. 19
77	longifolius	Lam.	long leaved	Europe	1800	......	Swt. Cist.
78	ledon	Lam.	ledon gum.	France	1730	......	Daham Arb. 1, 66
79	populifolius	Lin.	poplar leaved	Spain	1656	......	Swt. Cist. 23
80	laurifolius	Lin.	laurel leaved	......	1731	......	Swt. Cist. 52
81	Cyprius	Lam.	cyprus	Greece	1800	peat and loam	Swt. Cist. 39
	stenophyllus. Link. *ladaniferus*. B. M.						
82	cupanianus	Presl.	Cupani's	Sicily		sand and loam	Swt. Cist. 70.
83	acutifolius	Swt.	acute leaved	S. Europe		......	
	salvifolius ⎱ De Cand. *2 humifusus* ⎰						

HELIANTHEMUM Tourn.   Sun rose.

(Sect. 1. *Peduncles 1—3 flowered axillary, solitary, or umbellate, rarely paniculate.*)

No.	Systematic Name.	Authority.	English Name.	Native Country.	Time of Introd.	Soil.	Where figured.
84	umbellatum	Mil.	umbel leaved	S. Europe	1731	peat and loam	Swt. Cist. 5
	Cistus umbellatus Lin.						
85	Algarvense	Dunal.	Algarve	Portugal	1800	......	Bot. Mag. 627
	Cistus algarvensis B. M.						
86	formosum	Dunal.	beautiful	Portugal	1780	......	Swt. Cist. 50
	Cistus formosus Curt.						
87	candidum	Swt.	white leaved	Spain		......	Swt. Cist.

(Sect. 2, *Pedicels one flowered, before flowering drooping, during flowering erect, after flowering bent back.*)

No.	Systematic Name.	Authority.	English Name.	Native Country.	Time of Introd.	Soil.	Where figured.
88	procumbens	Dunal.	procumbent	S. Europe		sand and peat	Bar. ic 445
89	lævipes	Willd.	smooth footed	France	1690	......	Swt. Cist. 24
90	Barrelieri	Ten.	Barrelier's	Italy	1820	......	Bar. ic. 416

(Sect. 3. *Pedicels bracteate at the base.*)

No.	Systematic Name.	Authority.	English Name.	Native Country.	Time of Introd.	Soil.	Where figured.
91	Ælandicum	De Cand.	Æland.	Germany	1816	......	Swt. Cist. 2
	Cistus Ælandicus Lin.						
92	alpestre	Dunal.	alp.	Germany	1818	sand and loam	Crn. Aust. 6, 1.
93	Italicum	Pers.	Italian	Italy	1799	sand and peat	Bar. ic. 366
	Cistus Italicus Lin.						
94	marifolium	De Cand.	marum leaved	Britain		......	Eng. Bot. 396
	Cistus marifolius Lin.						

(Sect. 4. *Calyx before flowering somewhat twisted at the apex.*)

No.	Systematic Name.	Authority.	English Name.	Native Country.	Time of Introd.	Soil.	Where figured.
95	vulgare	Gært.	common	Britain		sand and loam	Eng. Bot. 1321
96	1 fol. variegatum		variegated leaves			......	
97	2 flor. pleno		double flowered			......	
98	3 aurantiacum					......	
99	flor. pleno					......	
100	4 sanguineum					......	
101	5 roseum					......	
102	Surrejanum	Mill.	Surrey	England		......	Eng. Bot. 2207
	Cistus Surrejanus Lin.						
103	grandiflorum	De Cand.	large flowered	Spain	1800	sand and peat	Scop. Carn. 25
	Cistus grandiflorus Scop.						
104	1 rubrum		red flowered			......	
105	2 sulphureum		sulphur-col. flwd.			......	
106	Apennine	De Cand.	Apennine	Italy	1731	......	Swt. Cist. 62
	Cistus Apenninus Lin.						
107	1 luteum		yellow flowered			......	
108	2 flor. pleno		double flowered			......	
109	mutabile	Pers.	changeable	S. Europe		sand and loam	Jacq. ic. 1, 99
	Cistus mutabilis Jacq.						
110	1 luteum		yellow flowered			......	
111	2 roseum	Swt.	rose flowered			......	
112	polifolium	De Cand.	polium leaved	England Downs		sand and peat	Eng. Bot. 1392
113	hyssopifolium	Ten.	hyssop leaved	Italy		sand and loam	
114	pulverulentum	De Cand.	powdered	France		......	Swt. Cist. 49
	Cistus polifolius Lam.		polium leaved				
115	Andersoni	Swt.	Anderson's	S. Europe		com. gard.	Swt. Cist. 90
116	stamineum	Swt.	straw coloured	Europe		......	Swt. Cist. 94
117	*multiplex 2 var.* ⎱ Swt. *macranthum* ⎰					......	
118	crocatum Swt. ⎱ *4 var.* hysso- ⎰ Ten. pifolium ⎰						
119	cupreum	Swt.	copper flowered	hybrids.		......	Swt. Cist. 60

Order, POLYGALEÆ. Juss. Ann. Mus. 14. 386.   Class, DIADELPHIA. Order, OCTANDRIA. Lin.

No.	Systematic Name.	Authority.	English Name.	Native Country.	Time of Introd.	Soil.	Where figured.
	POLYGALA	Tourn	Milk-wort				
120	Chamæbuxus	Lin.	bastard box	Austria	1658	sand and loam	Bot. Mag. 316

Order, MALVACEÆ. Brown.   Class, MONADELPHIA. Order, POLYANDRIA. Lin.

No.	Systematic Name.	Authority.	English Name.	Native Country.	Time of Introd.	Soil.	Where figured.
	HIBISCUS	Lin.					
121	Syriacus	Lin.	Syrian	Syria	1596	com. gard.	Bot. Mag. 83

No.	Systematic Name.	Authority.	English Name.	Native Country.	Time of Introd.	Soil.	Where figured.
	HIBISCUS.						
122	1 albo-plenus		double white			com. gard.	
123	2 carneo-plenus		double flesh-col.			......	
124	3 rubro-plenus		double red			.....	
125	4 violaceo-plenus		double violet			.....	
126	5 folio-variegatus		variegated leaved			......	

Order, TILIACEÆ. Juss. Gen. p. 290. Class, POLYANDRIA. Order, MONOGYNIA. Lin.

TILIA Lin. Lime tree

(*Sect. 1. Petals naked. Species all European.*)

No.	Systematic Name.	Authority.	English Name.	Native Country.	Time of Introd.	Soil.	Where figured.
127	microphylla	Vent.	small leaved	Britain		com. gard.	Eng. Bot. 1705
	parvifolia. Ehrh.						
128	platyphylla	Scop.	broad leaved			......	Vent. Til. 1, 2
	Europæa. Desf. *Cordata.* Mill. *Grandiflora. Ehrh.*						
129	1 aurea					......	
130	2 laciniata	Mill.	jagged leaf	Britain		......	
131	corallina	H. K.	coral			......	

(*Sect. 2. Petals inwardly with a scale at the base. Species chiefly American.*)

No.	Systematic Name.	Authority.	English Name.	Native Country.	Time of Introd.	Soil.	Where figured.
132	glabra	Vent.	smooth	N. America	1752	......	Wat. Den. Br. 134
	Americana. Lin. *Canadensis.* Michx.						
133	pubescens	Ait.	pubescent	......	1726	......	Wat. Den. Br. 135
	Caroliniana. Mill. *Americana.* Walth.						
134	heterophylla	Vent.	various leaved	......	1811	......	Vent. Til. 5
	alba	Michx.					

Order, TERNSTRŒMIACEÆ. De Cand. Class, MONADELPHIA. Order, POLYANDRIA. Lin.

Tribe V. *Gordonieæ.*

No.	Systematic Name.	Authority.	English Name.	Native Country.	Time of Introd.	Soil.	Where figured.
	STEWARTIA	Cav.					
135	Virginica	Cav.	Virginian	......	1742	loam and peat	Bot. Repos. 397
	Malachodendron. Lin. *Marylandica.* Andr.						
	GORDONIA	Ellis					
136	pubescens	Pursh	pubescent	......	1774	sand and peat	Ven. Mal. 1. .
	Lacathea florida Salisb.						

Order, HYPERICINEÆ. De Cand. Theor. ed. 1. p. 214. Class, POLYADELPHIA. Order, POLYANDRIA. Lin.

Tribe II. *Hypericeæ.* Chois. prod. hyp. p. 37.

HYPERICUM Lin. St. John's wort

(*Sect. 1. Sepals joined at the base, and unequal.*)

No.	Systematic Name.	Authority.	English Name.	Native Country.	Time of Introd.	Soil.	Where figured.
137	elatum	Ait.	tall	N. America	1762	sand and loam	Wat. Den. Br. 85
138	hircinum	Lin.	goat scented	S. Europe	1640	......	Wat. Den. Br. 86
139	———— minor						
140	floribundum	Ait.	bundle flowered	Madeira	1779	peat and loam	Com. h. 2, 68
141	Kalmianum	Lam.	Kalms	N. America	1759	sand and loam	
142	calycinum	Lin.	large calyxed	Ireland		com. gard.	Eng. Bot. 2017

(*Sect. 2. Sepals equal.*)

No.	Systematic Name.	Authority.	English Name.	Native Country.	Time of Introd.	Soil.	Where figured.
143	rosmarinifolium	Lam.	rosemary leaved	Carolina	1812	loam and peat	

Order, ACERINEÆ. De Cand. Theor. el. ed. 2. p. 244. Class, POLYGAMIA. Order, MONŒCIA, Lin.

(*Sect. 1. Flowers racemose.*)

No.	Systematic Name.	Authority.	English Name.	Native Country.	Time of Introd.	Soil.	Where figured.
	ACER	Mœnch	Maple.				
144	Tataricum	Lin.	Tartarian	Tartary	1759	com. gard.	Wat. Den. Br. 160
145	striatum	Lam.	striated	N. America	1755	......	Michx. Arb. 2, 17
	Pensylvanicum Lin. *Canadense* Duham.						
146	Pseudo-platanus	Lin.	sycamore	Britain		......	Eng. Bot. 303
147	1 fol. argentiis		silvery leaved			......	
148	2 fol. aurcis		golden leaved			......	
149	3 lutescens		yellow			......	
150	hybridum	Bosc.	hybrid			......	
151	montanum	Ait.	mountain	N. America	1750	sand and loam	Schm. ar. 1, 12
152	macrophyllum	Pursh.	long leaved	......	1826	com. gard.	
153	campestre	Lin.	field			.....	
154	fol. variegatis					......	
155	1 hebecarpon					......	

(*Sect. 2. Flowers corymbose, or fasiculate.*)

No.	Systematic Name.	Authority.	English Name.	Native Country.	Time of Introd.	Soil.	Where figured.
156	Opalus	Ait.	Opalus	Italy	1752	......	
	rotundifolium. Lam. *Italum.* Lauth.						
157	Opalifolium	Vill.	Guelder rose lvd.	S. France	1823	......	Trat. ar. 1, 13, ic.
158	Creticum	Lin.	Cretan	Levant	1752	......	Schm. ar. 15
159	Monspessulanum	Lin.	Montpelier	France	1739	......	Schm. ar. 1, 14
	trifolium. Duham. *trilobum.* Mœnch.						
160	Ibericum	Beib.	Iberian	Iberia		......	
161	barbatum	Michx.	bearded	N. America	1812	......	
	Carolinianum Walt.						
162	platanoides	Lin.	plantain-like	Europe	1683	......	Schm. 1, 3, 4
163	2 crispum	Lauth.				......	
164	saccharinum	Lin.	sugar	N. America	1735	......	Michx. arb. 2, 15
165	dasycarpon	Willd.	hairy fruited	......	1725	......	Michx. arb. 2, 13
	floridanum Hort.						

eriocarpon. Michx. *Sanguineum.* Hort.

No.	Systematic Name.	Authority.	English Name.	Native Country.	Time of Introd.	Soil.	Where figured.
	ACER						
166	rubrum coccineum	Lin.	red	N. America	1656	com. gard.	Michx. arb. 2, 14

(Sect. 3. *Umbels pedunculate.*)

No.	Systematic Name.	Authority.	English Name.	Native Country.	Time of Introd.	Soil.	Where figured.
167	palmatum	Thunb.	palmate	Japan	1820	......	Trat. ar. 1, 17, ic.
168	lævigatum	Wall	smooth leaved	Nepaul		......	Wall. Pl. As. 2, 3. t. 104

NEGUNDO Mœnch Box elder   Class, DIŒCIA. Order, HEXEMDRIA. Lin.

No.	Systematic Name.	Authority.	English Name.	Native Country.	Time of Introd.	Soil.	Where figured.
169	fraxinifolium *Acer negundo*	Nutt Lin.	ash leaved	N. America	1688	......	Schm. ar. 1, 12

Order, HIPPOCASTANEÆ. De Cand. Theor. ed. 2. 244.   Class, HEPTANDRIA. Order, MONOGYNIA. Lin.

No.	Systematic Name.	Authority.	English Name.	Native Country.	Time of Introd.	Soil.	Where figured.
	ÆSCULUS	Lin.	Horsechesnut				
170	hippocastanum	Lin.	common	Asia	1629	......	Schm. ar. 1, 38
171	1 fol. argenteis					......	
172	2 fol. aureis					......	
173	rubicunda	De Cand.	ruddy	N. America	1820	......	Wat. Den. Br. 121
174	glabra	Willd.	smooth leaved	......	1812	......	
	PAVIA	Boer.					
175	macrostachya *Æsculus parviflora.* Walt. *Pavia edulis.* Poir.	De Cand.	long spiked	......	1830	......	Col. h. Rip. 19
176	rubra *Æsculus pavia.* Lin.	Lam.	red flowered	......	1711	......	Wat. Den. Br. 120
177	hybrida *Æsculus discolor.* Pursh. *Æsculus discolor.* De Cand.	De Cand.	hybrid	......	1812	......	
178	humilis *Æsculus humilis* Lod.	G. Don.	low	......		......	Bot. Reg 1018
179	flava *Æsculus flava.* Ait. *Pavia lutea.* Poir.	De Cand.	yellow	......	1764	......	Wat. Den. Br. 163
180	aculeata					......	

Order, SAPINDACEÆ. Juss. Ann. 18. p. 476.   Class, OCTANDRIA. Order, MONOGYNIA. Lin.

Tribe III. *Dodonæaceæ.* Humbt. and Kunth.

No.	Systematic Name.	Authority.	English Name.	Native Country.	Time of Introd.	Soil.	Where figured.
	KÖLREUTERIA	Lax					
181	paniculata *paulinioides*	Lax L'Her.	panicled	China	1763	......	Bot. Reg. 320

Order, AMPELIDEÆ. Humbt. and Kunth.   Class, PENTANDRIA. Order, MONOGYNIA. Lin.

Tribe I. *Viniferæ seu Sarmentaceæ.*

No.	Systematic Name.	Authority.	English Name.	Native Country.	Time of Introd.	Soil.	Where figured.
	VITIS	Lin.					
182	vinifera	Lin.	vine bearing	various		rich mould	Jacq. ic. 1, 50
183	Labrusca	Lin.	wild vine	N. America	1656	sand and peat	Jacq. Sch. 426
184	cordifolia *incisa* Jacq. *Vulpina,* Walt.	Michx.	heart-shaped lvd.	......	1806	......	Jacq. Sch. 427
185	riparia *odoratissima*	Michx.	river bank	......	1806	sand and loam	Bot. Mag. 2429
186	Æstivalis *vulpina*	Michx. Willd.	summer	......	1656	sand and peat	Jacq. Sch. 425
187	1 fructu albâ		white fruited			rich mould	
188	2 fructu nigrâ		black fruited			......	
189	3 fructu rubrâ		red fruited			......	
	AMPELOPSIS	Michx.					

(Sect. 1. *Leaves palmate.*)

No.	Systematic Name.	Authority.	English Name.	Native Country.	Time of Introd.	Soil.	Where figured.
190	hederacea *Vitis quinquifolia,* Lam. *Cissus quinquifolia,* Purst. *Vitis hederacea,* Willd.	Michx.	Ivy-like	N. America	1629	com. gard.	Cor. Can. 100
191	hirsuta	Don.	hairy	......	1806	......	

(Sect. 2. *Leaves pinnate or bipinnate.*)

No.	Systematic Name.	Authority.	English Name.	Native Country.	Time of Introd.	Soil.	Where figured.
192	bipinnata *Vitis arborea* Willd. *Cissus stans.* Pers.	Michx.	bipinnate	......	1700	......	Ac. Bon. 3, 24

Order, RUTACEÆ. Juss. Gen. 296.   Class, DECANDRIA. Order, MONOGYNIA. Lin.

Tribe 1. *Diosmeæ.*

No.	Systematic Name.	Authority.	English Name.	Native Country.	Time of Introd.	Soil.	Where figured.
	RUTA	Tourn.					
193	graveolens *hortensis*	Lin. Mill.	heavy-scented	S. Europe	1561	com. gard.	Duham 2, 61 Lam. il 345
194	divaricata	Ten.	divaricate	Italy	1820	......	
	ZANTHOXYLUM	Humbt. and Kunth.					
195	Virginicum	Lod.	Virginian			sand and loam	
196	fraxineum	Willd.	Ash leaved	N. America	1759	......	Duham Arb. 1, 97

Order, CORIARIEÆ. De Cand. Prod. vol. 1. p. 739.   Class, DIŒCIA. Order, DECANDRIA. Lin.

No.	Systematic Name.	Authority.	English Name.	Native Country.	Time of Introd.	Soil.	Where figured.
	CORIARIA	Lin.					
197	myrtifolia	Lin.	Myrtle leaved	S. Europe	1629	com. gard.	Wat. Den. Br. 103

Order, CELASTRINEÆ. Brown.   Class, PENTANDRIA. Order, TRIGYNIA. Lin.

Tribe I. *Staphyleaceæ.* De Cand.

No.	Systematic Name.	Authority.	English Name.	Native Country.	Time of Introd.	Soil.	Where figured.
	STAPHYLEA	Lin.	Bladder nut				
198	trifolia	Lin.	three leaved	N. America	1640	......	Schm. Arb. 80
199	pinnata *Staphylodendron pinnatum,* Scop.	Lin.	pinnate leaved	England		......	Eng. Bot. 1560

B

No.	Systematic Name.	Authority.	English Name.	Native Country.	Time of Introd.	Soil.	Where figured.

Tribe II. *Evonymeæ.* De Cand.

	EVONYMUS	Tourn.	Spindle tree	Class, PENTANDRIA. Order, MONOGYNIA. Lin.			
200	Europæus	Lin.	Europæan	Britain		com. gard.	Eng. Bot. 392

(Sect. 1. *Petals oblong or ovate, species Europæan.*)

Euonymus vulgaris, Mill.

201	1 fol. variegatis					......	
202	2 fructu albâ					......	
203	verrucosus	Scop.	warted	Austria	1763	sand and loam	Schm. Arb. 72
	leprosus	Lin. fil.					
204	latifolius	Bauh.	broad leaved	......	1730	......	Bot. Mag. 2384
	europæus	Lin.					
205	nanus	Bieb.	dwarf	Caucasus	1825	......	

(Sect. 2. *Petals orbiculate, species American.*)

206	atropurpureus	Jacq.	dark purple	N. America	1756	peat and loam	Schm. Arb. 73
	Carolinensis	Marsh					
207	Americanus	Lin.	American	......	1683	sand and peat	Schm. Arb. 75
	semperrivens	Marsh.	*alternifolius,* Mœnch.				
208	angustifolius	Pursh.	narrow leaved	......	1806	peat and loam	
	CELASTRUS	Lin.	Staff Tree				
209	scandens	Lin.	climbing	......	1736	sand and loam	Schk. han. 1, 47
210	obovatus	Lod.	obovate			......	

Tribe III. *Aquifoliaceæ.* De Cand.

	ILEX	Lin.	Holly	Class, TETRANDRIA. Order, TETRAGYNIA. Lin.			
211	aquifolium	Lin.	prickly leaved	Britain		com. gard.	Eng. Bot. 496
212	1 heterophylla		various leaved	......			
213	2 crassifolia		thick leaved				
214	3 recurva		recurved				
215	4 serratifolia		serrate leaved				
216	5 ciliata		ciliate leaved				
217	6 ciliata minor		small ciliate lvd.				
218	7 ferox		fierce				
219	8 latifolia		broad leaved				
220	9 laurifolia		laurel leaved				
221	10 marginata		marginate				
222	11 fol. argentiis		silvery leaved				
223	12 fol. aureis		golden leaved				
224	13 fructu luteâ		yellow fruited				
225	14 var						
226	15 var						
227	16 var						
228	17 var						
229	18 var						
230	19 var						
231	20 var						
232	21 var						
233	22 var						
234	23 var						
235	24 var						
236	25 var						
237	26 var						
238	27 var						
239	28 var						
240	29 var						
241	30 var						
242	31 var						
243	32 var						
244	33 var						
245	34 var						
246	35 var						
247	36 var						
248	37 var						
249	38 var						
250	39 var						
251	40 var						
252	41 var						
253	balearica	Desf.	Balearic	Minorca	1815	com. gard	
254	perado	H. K.	Perado	Madeira	1760	sand and loam	Meerb. ic. 2 t 6
	Maderensis	Lam.					
255	opaca	Ait.	opaque	N. America	1744	peat and loam	Meerb. ic. 2 t 5
	quercifolia	Meerb.					
256	dahoon	Walt.	Dahoon	Carolina	1726	sand and loam	
	cassine	Willd.					
257	cassine	Ait.	Cassine	......	1726	......	Cat. Car. 2, 57
	Aquifolium Carolinense, Cat. car.						
	Caroliniana	Mill.					
258	vomitoria	Ait.	emetic	......	1700	com. gard.	Cat. Car. 2, 57

No.	Systematic Name.	Authority.	English Name.	Native Country.	Time of Introd.	Soil.	Where figured.
	PRINOS	Lin.			Class, HEXANDRIA. Order, MONOGYNIA. Lin.		

(Sect. 1. *Flowers frequently with four or five divisions.*)

No.	Systematic Name.	Authority.	English Name.	Native Country.	Time of Introd.	Soil.	Where figured.
259	deciduus	De Cand.	deciduous	N. America	1760	sand and loam	
	Ilex decidua.	Walt.	*Ilex prinoides*, Ait. hort. Kew.				
260	ambiguus	Michx.	ambiguous	......	1812	......	Wat. Den. Br. 29
	Cassine Caroliniana. Walt.						

(Sect. 2. *Flowers frequently with six divisions, leaves falling off.*)

261	verticillatus	Lin.	whorled	Canada	1736	sand and peat	Wat. Den. Br. 30
	padifolius	Willd.	*Gronovii*, Michx. *confertus*, Mœnch.				
262	laevigatus	Pursh.	smooth	N. America		......	Wat. Den. Br. 28
263	lanceolatus	Pursh.	lance leaved	......	1811	......	

(Sect. 3. *Flowers frequently with six divisions, leaves not falling off.*)

264	glaber	Lin.	smooth	Canada		sand and loam	
265	prunifolius	Desf.	Plum leaved	N. America	1810	sand and peat	
	NEMOPANTHUS	Rafn.			Class, DIŒCIA. Order, HEXANDRIA. Lin.		
266	Canadensis	De Cand.	Canadian	N. America	1812	peat and loam	De Cand. Gen. 3
	facicularis	Rafn.	*Ilex canadensis*, Michx. *delicatula*, Bart.				

Order, RHAMNEÆ. Brown. Class, PENTANDRIA. Order, MONOGYNIA. Lin.

267	ZIZIPHUS vulgaris	Tourn. Lam.	common	S. Europe	1640	loam and peat	Pal. Ross. 2 t 59
	Rhamnus Zizyphus. Lin.						
268	PALIURUS aculeatus	Tourn. Lam.	Christ's Thorn pointed	......	1596	com. gard.	Lam. il. 210
	petasus	Dum.	*Australis*, Gœrtn. *vulgaris*, Don. *Rhamnus paliunus. Ziziphus paliurus*, Willd.				
269	BERCHEMIA volubilis	Neck. De Cand.	twining	Carolina	1714	sand and peat	Jacq. ic. 2, 336
	Rhamnus volubilis, Lin. *Ziziphus volubilis*, Willd. *Œnoplia volubilis*, Schult.						
	RHAMNUS	Lam.	Buckthorn				

(Sect. 1. *Branches without thorns, leaves smooth, leathery, not falling off.*)

270	alaternus	Lin.	bast. lvd. alater	S. Europe	1629	com. gard.	Duham Arb. t. 14
	Alaternus Phylica. Mill.						
271	1 fol. aureis				......		
272	2 fol. laciniatis				......		
273	3 fol. variegatis				......		
274	hybridus	L'her.	hybrid		......		Her. Ser. 5
	Burgundicus, Hort. Par. *sempervirum*, Hort.						
275	Clusii	Willd.	Clusius'	S. Europe	1629	......	

(Sect. 2. *Branches terminating in a thorn, leaves falling off.*)

276	Catharticus	Lin.	purging	England		......	Eng. Bot. 1629
277	1 latifolius		broad leaved				
278	infectorius	Lin.	dyers	S. Europe	1683	......	Ard. m. 78, 14
279	tinctorius	Waldst.	dyers	Hungary	1820	......	Waldst. Kit. 2, 55
	Cardiocarpus	Willd.					
280	saxatilis	Lin.	rock	Europe	1752	......	Jacq. Aust. 1, 53
281	theezans	Lin.	Theesan tea	China		......	
	Rhamnus Thea. Osbeck.						

(Sect. 3. *Branches without thorns, leaves falling off.*)

282	alpinus	Lin.	alpine	Switzerland	1752	......	Hall. Hist. t 60
283	alnifolius	L'her.	Alder leaved	N. America	1778	......	
284	frangula	Lin.	frangula	Britain		......	Eng. Bot. 250
285	latifolius	L'her.	broad leaved	Azores	1778	......	Wat. Den. Br. 11

Order, HOMALINEÆ. Brown. Cong. p. 19. Class, DODECANDRIA. Order, MONOGYNIA. Lin.

286	ARISTOTELIA Macqui	L'her. Lin. Poir.	Macqui	Chile	1733	......	Wat. Den. Br. 44
	glandulosa	Poir.					
287	1 fol. variegatis				......		

Order, TEREBINTACEÆ. Juss. Gen. 368. Class, PENTANDRIA. Order, TRIGYNIA. Lin.

Tribe II. *Sumachineæ.* De Cand.

	RHUS	Lin.	Sumach				

(Sect. 1. *Leaves many paired, with an odd one.*)

288	typhina	Lin.	fever	N. America	1629	......	Wat. Den. Br. 17, 18
289	1 erecta						
290	viridiflora	Poir.	green flowered	......			
	Canadensis	Mill.					
291	glabra	Lin.	smooth	......	1726	......	Dil. Elth. 243—314
292	1 elegans	Ait.					
293	copallina	Lin.	gum copal	......	1688	peat and loam	Jacq. Sch. 3, 341
294	venata	De Cand.	poison	......	1713	com. gard.	Wat. Den. Br. 19
295	chinensis	Mill.	Chinese	China	1800	peat and loam	

No.	Systematic Name.	Authority.	English Name.	Native Country.	Time of Introd.	Soil.	Where figured.

RHUS.

(Sect. 2. Leaves one pair, with an odd one.)

296	radicans	Lin.	rooting	N. America	1724	peat and loam	Bot. Mag. 1806
297	toxicodendron	Lin.	poison oak	......	1640	com. gard.	
298	suaveolens	Ait.	sweet smelling	......		peat and loam	
	Toxicodendron crenatum. Mill.						
299	trifoliata		three leaved			com. gard.	

(Sect. 3. Leaves simple.)

| 300 | cotinus | Lin. | wild olive | S. Europe | 1656 | ...... | Jacq. Aust. t. 238 |
| | *Cotinus coggygria.* Scop. et Mœnch. | | | | | | |

Tribe VI. *Pteleaceæ.* Kunth.

PTELEA		Lin.	Shrubby Trefoil	Class, TETRANDRIA. Order, MONOGYNIA. Lin.			
301	trifoliata	Lin.	three leaved	N. America	1704	......	Dil. Elth. 122
CNEORUM		Lin.	Widow wail	Class, TRIANDRIA. Order, MONOGYNIA. Lin.			
302	tricoccon	Lin.	three grained	Spain	1793	peat and loam	Lam. il. 27

Tribe VII. *Connaraceæ.* Brown.

AILANTUS		Desf.		Class, POLYGANICA. Order, DIŒCIA. Lin.			
303	glandulosa	Desf.	glandulous	China	1751	com. gard.	Wat. Den. Br. 104
	procera	Sal.	*Rhus hypsolodendron,* Mœnch. *Rhus cacodendron,* Erhr.				

Order, LEGUMINOSÆ. Juss. Gen. 345. Class, DECANDRIA. Order, MONOGYNIA. Lin.

Sub-Order, PAPILIONACEÆ. Lin. Tribe I. *Sophoreæ.* Spreng.

SOPHORA		Brown					
304	japonica	Lin.	Japanese	Japan	1763	sand and loam	Bot. Reg. 585
	Sinica	Rosier					
305	macrocarpa	Smith	large fruited	Chili	1822	......	
EDWARDSIA		Salisb.					
306	microphylla	Salisb.	small leaved	New Zealand	1772	sand and peat	Bot. Mag. 1442
	Sophora microphylla, Ait. *Sophora tetraptera,* Lin.						
VIRGILIA		Lam.					
307	lutea	Michx.	yellow flowered	N. America	1812	peat and loam	Michx. arb. t. 3
PIPTANTHUS		Swt.					
308	Nepalensis	Swt.	Nepal	Nepal	1821	com. gard.	Swt. Fl. Gar. 264

Tribe II. *Loteæ.* De Cand. Prod. p. 115. Sub-Tribe I. *Genisteæ.* Bronn Diss.

ULEX		Lin.	FURZE	Class DIADELPHIA. Order, DECANDRIA. Lin.			
309	Europæus	Lin.	Europe	Britain		......	Eng. Bot. t. 742
	grandiflorus	Pourr.	*vernalis,* Thore.				
310	var. flor. pleno					......	
311	strictus		upright		......		
312	nanus	Smith	drawf.	......		......	
	Autumnalis	Thore.	*minor,* Roth.				
SPARTIUM		De Cand.	Broom			......	Eng. Bot. t. 743
313	junceum	Lin.	rush	S. Europe		......	Bot. Mag. 85
	Genista juncea	Lam.	*Genista odorata,* Mœnch. *Spartianthus junceus,* Link.				
GENISTA		Lam.					

(Sect. 1. Branches unarmed, leaves mostly trifoliate.)

314	candicans	Lin.	whitish	Spain	1735	sand and loam	Wat. Den. Br. 80
	Cytisus candicans, Lin. *Cytisus pubescens,* Mœnch.						
315	triquetra	Ait.	triangular	Corsica	1770	sand and peat	Bot. Mag. 314
316	var. flor. pleno.						
317	radiata	Scop.	rayed	Italy	1758	......	Bot. Mag. 2260
	Spartium radiatum, Lin. *Genista Ilvensis,* Dalech.						

(Sect. 2. Branches spiny, leaves mostly trifoliate.)

| 318 | ephedroides | De Cand. | ephedra like | Sardinia | 1832 | ...... | Maund's Bot. Gard. |

(Sect. 3. Branches, spiny, leaves simple.)

319	scorpius	De Cand.	scorpion	S. Europe	1570	peat and loam	Wat. Den. Br. 78
	Spartium scorpius, Lin. *Genista spiniflora,* Lam.						
320	Anglica	Lin.	English petty whin.	Britain		com. gard.	Eng. Bot. t. 133
	Genista minor	Lam.					
321	Germanica	Lin.	German	Germany	1773	......	
	Scorpius spinosus, Mœnch. *Voglera spinosa,* Fl. Wett.						

(Sect. 4. Branches unarmed, leaves simple.)

322	purgans	Lin.	purging	S. France	1768	peat and loam	Bul. her. 115
	Spartium purgans Lin.						
323	scariosa	Viv.	scarious	Italy	1821	com. gard.	
	Genista Januensis, Viv. *Genista Genuensis,* Pers.						
324	Anxantica	Ten.	Anxantic	......	1818	sand and loam	Fl. Nap. 2, 66
325	tinctoria	Lin.	dyers	Britain		com. gard.	Eng. Bot. t. 44
	Genistoides tinctoria Moench						
326	Sibirica	Lin.	Siberian	Siberia	1785	......	Jacq. Vin. 2, 190
	Genistoides elata Moench						

No.	Systematic Name.	Authority.	English Name.	Native Country.	Time of Introd.	Soil.	Where figured
	GENISTA.						
327	ovata	Waldst.	ovate	Italy	1816	com. gard.	Waldst. & Kit. ic. 84
328	sagittalis	Lin.	arrow jointed	Europe	1570	......	Jacq. Aust. 3, 209
	herbacea Lam. *Genistella racemosa* Mœnch. *Saltzwedelia sagittalis* Fl. Wett.						
329	prostrata	Lam.	prostrate	......	1816	......	
	pedunculata L'her. *decumbens* Willd. *Halleri* Reyn.						
330	pillosa	Lin.	hairy	Britain		sand and loam	Eng. Bot. t. 308
	repens Lam. *Genistoides tuberculata,* Mœnch. *Spartium pilosum* Roth.						
	CYTISUS	De Cand.					

(Sect. 1. *Calyx campanulate, legume few seeded, flowers white, leaves few, branches unarmed.*)

331	albus	Link.	white	Lusitania	1752	com. gard.	Duham Arb. 23
	Genista alba Lam. *Spartium album* Desf. *Spartium multiflorum* Ait.						
332	1 incarnata						

(Sect. 2. *Calyx campanulate, legume many seeded, branches unarmed leafy.   Flowers yellow.*)

333	Laburnum	Lin.	Laburnum	Austria	1596	......	Bot. Mag. 176
334	1 fol. variegatis		variegated lvd.				
335	2 fol. incisis		jagged leaved				
336	3 fol. pendulis		pendulous				
337	4 flor. purpureis		purple flowered				
338	alpinus	Mill.	Alpine	Europe	1596	......	
	angustifolius	Mœnch					
339	nigricans	Lin.	black rooted	......	1731	......	Bot. Reg. 802
340	sessilifolius	Lin.	sessile leaved	Italy	1713	......	Bot. Mag. 255
341	triflorus	L'her.	three flowered	Spain	1640	......	
	villosus	Pourr.					
342	scoparius	Link.	Broom	England		......	Eng. Bot. 1339
	Spartium scoparium Lin. *Genista scoparia* Lam. *Genista hirsuta* Mœnch.						
343	1 flor. albis						
344	2 fol. variegatis						

(Sect. 3. *Calyx tubulose, branches unarmed.   Flowers white, purple, or yellow.*)

345	purpureus	Scop.	purple	Austria	1792	sandy loam	Bot. Mag. 1176
346	biflorus	L'her.	two flowered	Hungary	1760	com. gard.	Bot. Reg. 308
	supinus Jacq. *hirsutus* Gmel. *hirsutus et supinus* Beib. *macrospermus* Bess.						
347	elongatus	Waldst.	long branched	......	1804	......	Waldst. & Kit. 2. 183
348	2 multiflorus	De Cand.	many flowered				
349	3 decumbens	Lod.	decumbent				
350	falcatus	Waldst.	sickle shaped	......	1816	......	Bot. Cab. 520
351	ruthenicus	Fisch.	Russian	Russia	1817	......	
352	capitatus	Jacq.	capitate	Austria	1774	......	Bot. Cab. 497
	supinus Lin. *hirsutus* Lam.						
353	1 minor						
354	polytricus	Beib.	much-haired	Tauria	1818	sandy loam	

(Sect. 4. *Branches decumbent, tube of the calyx short obconic, corolla scarcely longer than the calyx. Flowers yellow subcapitate.*)

355	calycinus	Beib.	large calyxed	Caucasus	1820	......	Bot. Cab. 673
	pauciflorus Willd. *nanus* Willd.						
	ADENOCARPUS	De Cand.					
356	foliolosus	De Cand.	leafy	Canaries	1779	......	Bot. Mag. 42
	Cytisus foliolosus Ait.						
	ONONIS	Lin.					
357	rotundifolia	Lin.	round leaved	Pyrenees	1570	loam and peat	Bot. Mag. 335
	latifolia Asso. *Natrix rotundifolia* Mœnch.						
358	fruticosa	Lin.	shrubby	South of France	1748	peat	Bot. Mag. 317
	Natrix fruticosa Mœnch.						

Sub-Tribe IV.   *Galegeæ.*   Bronn.

	AMORPHA	Lin.	Bastard indigo				
359	fruticosa	Lin.	shrubby	Carolina	1724	loam and sand	Bot. Reg. 427
360	cerulæa	Lod.	blue flowered			......	
361	Lewisii	Lod	Lewis'	N. America	1820	......	
	LONCHOCARPUS	Humb. & Kunth.					
362	sepium	De Cand.	Hedge	West Indies	1821	......	
	Robinia sepium Jacq.						
	ROBINIA	De Cand.					
363	pseudacacia	Lin.	Bastard acacia	N. America	1640	com. gard.	Duham Arb. t. 16
	Pseudacacia odorata Mœnch. *Eschinomene pseudacacia* Roxb.						
364	2 inermis	Willd.	unarmed	......			
	spectabilis	Dum.		......			
365	3 crispa	De Cand.	curled	......			
366	5 tortuosa	De Cand.	twisted	......			
	hybrida Audib.	*ambigua* Poir.		......	1811	......	
367	dubia	Fouc.	doubtful	......			
368	monstrosa	Hort.	monstrous	......		......	
369	procera	Lod.	tall	......		......	
370	viscosa	Vent.	clammy	......	1797	......	Bot. Mag. 56
	glutinosa	Curt.					

c

No.	Systematic Name.	Authority.	English Name.	Native Country.	Time of Introd.	Soil.	Where figured.
	ROBINIA.	Lin.					
371	hispida	Lin.	hispid	Carolina	1742	com. gard. ►	Bot. Mag. 31
	rosea Duham.	*montana* Bart.	*Eschinomene hispida* Roxb.				
372	1 arborea		tree				
373	macrocantha	Lod.	long spiked			......	
	COLUTEA	Brown	Bladder senna				
374	arborescens	Lin.	arborescent	Europe	1570	......	Bot. Mag. 81
	hirsuta	Roth.					
375	cruenta	Ait.	bloody	Levant	1731	......	Schm. Arb. 119
	orientalis Lam.	*sanguinea* Pall.	*aperta* Schmidt.				
376	Haleppica	Lam.	Aleppo	......	1752	......	Schm. Arb. 120
	Pocockii	Ait.					
	CARAGANA	Lam.	Siberian pea tree				
377	Altagana	Poir.	Altagna	Siberia	1789	loam and sand	
	Robinia Altagana Pall.	*Caragana microphylla* Lam.					
378	microphylla	De Cand.	small leaved	Russia	1819	......	
	Robinia microphylla Pall.						
379	arborescens	Lam.	arborescent	Siberia	1752	......	Schm. Arb. 1, 33
	Robinia caragana Lin.						
380	2 inermis		unarmed				
381	Chamlagu	Lam.	Chamlagu	China	1773	......	
	Robinia chamlagu L'her.						
382	pygmæa	De Cand.	pygmy	Siberia	1751	......	Schm. Arb. 1, 37
	Robinia pygmæa Lin.						
383	spinosa	De Cand.	thorny	......	1775	com. gard.	Bot. Reg 1021
	Robinia spinosa Lin.	*Robinia ferox* Pall.					

Sub-Tribe V. *Astragaleæ.* Adans.

	ASTRAGALUS	Lin.	Milk Vetch				

(Sect. 1. *Petioles distinct from the stipules, not spinescent.*)

384	fruticosus	Pall.	Shrubby	Siberia	1804	loam and peat	Pall. astr. 19

(Sect. 2. *Petioles adhering to the stipules, persistent, spinescent.*)

385	Tragacantha	Lin.	Great Goat thorn	S. Europe	1640	......	Wat. Den. Br. 84

Tribe III. *Hedysareæ.* De Cand. Sub-Tribe I. *Coronilleæ.* De Cand.

	CORONILLA						
386	emerus	Lin.	Scorpion Senna	France	1596	com. gard.	Bot. Mag. 445
	Emerus major Mill.	*Coronilla pauciflora* Lam.					

Tribe IV. *Vicieæ.* Bronn.

	LATHYRUS	Lin.					
387	Armitageanus	Westcott	Armitage	Brazil	1834	loam and peat	Maund's Bot. Gard.

Tribe V. *Phaseoleæ.* Bronn.

	WISTARIA	Nutt					
388	frutescens	De Cand.	shrubby	N. America	1724	......	Bot. Mag. 2103
	Glycine frutescens Lin.	*Apios frutescens* Pursh.	*Wistaria speciosa* Nutt.		*Thyrsanthus frutescens* El.		
389	chinensis	De Cand.	Chinese	China	1818	......	Bot. Mag. 2083
	Glycine chinensis Sims.	*Sinensis* Bot. Reg.					
	LUPINUS	Tourn.					
390	arboreus	Sims	tree	unknown	1793	sandy loam	Bot. Mag. 682

Tribe VIII. *Mimoseæ.* Brown.

	ACACIA	Neck.		Class, POLYGAMIA. Order, MONŒCIA. Lin.			
391	Julibrissin	Willd.	Silk tree	Levant	1745	......	
	Mimosa arborea Forsk.	*Mimosa julibrissin* Scop.					

Tribe X. *Cassieæ.* De Cand.

	GLEDITSCHIA	Lin.		Class, POLYGAMIA. Order, DIŒCIA. Lin.			
392	triacanthos	Lin.	honey locust	N. America	1700	com. gard.	Wat. Den. Br. 138
393	2 inermis	De Cand.	unarmed				
394	monosperma	Walt.	one seeded	......	1723	......	Cat. Car. 1, 43
	aquatica Marsh.	*carolinensis* Lam.	*triacantha* Gært.				
395	Sinensis	Lam.	Chinese	China	1774	......	Wat. Den. Br. 75
	horrida	Willd.					
396	1 major						
397	2 purpurea						
398	ferox	Desf.	fierce	......		......	
	orientalis	Bosc.					
399	macracantha	Desf.	long spined	......		......	
400	Caspica	Desf.	Caspian	Caspia	1822	......	
401	Javanica	Lam.	Javan	Java		......	
	GYMNOCLADUS	Lam.		Class, DIŒCIA. Order, DECANDRIA. Lin.			
402	Canadensis	Lam.	Canadian	Canada	1748	peat and loam	Michx. am. 2, 51
	Guilandina dioica Lin.						
	CERCIS	Lin.		Class, DECANDRIA. Order, MONOGYNIA. Lin.			
403	Siliquastrum	Lin.	Siliquastrum	S. Europe	1596	......	Bot. Mag. 1138
	Siliquastrum orbiculatum Mœnch.						

No.	Systematic Name.	Authority.	English Name.	Native Country.	Time of Introd.	Soil.	Where figured.
	CERCIS.						
404	Canadensis	Lin.	Canadian	Canada	1730	peat and loam	
	Siliquastrum cordatum Mœnch.						

Order, ROSACEÆ. Juss.   Class, ICOSANDRIA. Order, MONOGYNIA. Lin.

Tribe II. *Amygdaleæ.* Juss.

No.	Systematic Name.	Authority.	English Name.	Native Country.	Time of Introd.	Soil.	Where figured.
	AMYGDALUS	Tourn.	Almond				

(Sect. 1. *Calyxes cylindrical bell shaped.*)

| 405 | nana | Lin. | dwarf | Russia | 1683 | peat and loam | Bot. Mag. 161 |
| 406 | Sibirica | Lod. | Siberian | Siberia | 1820 | com. gard. | |

(Sect. 2. *Calyxes bell shaped.*)

407	communis	Lin.	common	Barbary	1570	......	Woodville Med. Bot. t. 83
408	1 amara	De Cand.	bitter			......	
409	Cochinchinensis	Lour.	Cochinchina	Cochin China		......	
	ARMENIACA	Tourn.	Apricot				
410	vulgaris	Lam.	common	Levant	1562	......	Lam. il. 431
	Prunus armeniaca Lin.						
411	1 flor. plen.		double flowered			......	
412	dasycarpa	Pers.	thick fruited		1800	......	Bot. Cab. 1250
	atropurpurea Lois. *Prunus dasycarpa* Ehrh. *Prunus armeniaca nigra* Desf.						
413	Sibirica	Pers.	Siberian	Siberia	1788 1819	......	Pall. Ross. 1, 8
	Prunus Sibirica Lin.						
414	Brigantiaca	Pers.	Brigantian	S. Europe		......	
	Prunus Brigantiaca Lin.						
	PRUNUS	Tourn.	Plum				
415	spinosa	Lin.	thorny	Britain		......	Eng. Bot. 842
	acacia Crantz. *sylvestris* Mill.						
416	pedunculata	Pall.	pedunculate	Dahuria	1833	loam and peat	
417	maritima	Wangenb.	sea shore	N. America	1800	com. gard.	
418	pubescens	Poir.	pubescent		1818	......	
419	domestica	Lin.	domestic	England		......	Eng. Bot. 1783
420	3 cerasifera	Ehrh.	cherry-like			......	
	myrobalana Desf. *mirobalana* Lois.						
421	polytricus	L. C.	many haired			......	
	CERASUS	Juss.	Cherry				

(Sect. 1. *Flowers umbellate.*)

422	Avium	Mœnch.	Birds	England		......	Eng. Bot. 706
	nigra Mill. (non Ait.) *Prunus cerasus avium* Lin.						
423	caproniana	De Cand.	capronian	S. Europe		......	
424	1 sem. pleno		half double			......	
425	nigra	Lois.	black fruited	N. America	1773	......	Bot. Mag. 1117
	nigra Ait.						
426	borealis	Michx.	northern	......	1822	......	
	Prunus borealis Poir.						
427	depressa	Pursh.	depressed	......	1805	......	
	pumila Michx. (non *Prunus pumila* Lin.) *Prunus Susquehannæ* Willd.						
428	chicasa	Michx.	Chicasaw	......	1806	......	

(Sect. 2. *Flowers racemose.*)

429	Pensylvanica	Lois.	Pensylvanian	......	1773	......	Willd. Arb. t. 3
	Prunus pensylvanica Lin. *Prunus lanceolata* Willd.						
430	Mahaleb	Mill.	Mahaleb	Austria	1714	......	Jacq. Aust. 3, 227
	Prunus Mahaleb Lin.						
431	1 fructu luteâ		yellow fruited			......	
432	padus	De Cand.	Bird cherry	Britain		......	Eng. Bot. 1383
	Prunus padus Lin.						
433	3 rubra					......	
434	virginiana	Michx.	Virginian	Virginia	1724	......	Willd. Arb. t. 5, f. 1
	Prunus arguta Bigelow						
435	scrotina	Lois.	evening	N. America	1629	......	Willd. Arb. t. 5, f. 2
	Prunus scrotina Willd. *Virginiana* Mill.						

(Sect. 3. *Leaves leathery, evergreen.*)

436	lusitanica	Lois.	Portugal laurel	Lusitania	1640	......	Mill. ic. t. 196, f. 1
	Prunus lusitanica Lin.						
437	Laurocerasus	Lois.	common laurel	Levant	1629	......	Woodville Med. Bot. t. 230
	Prunus laurocerasus Lin.						
438	1 fol. variegatis		variegated leaved			......	
439	2 angustifolia		narrow leaved			......	
440	3 longifolia		long leaved			......	
441	Coroliniana	Michx.	Carolinian	Carolina	1759	......	

Tribe III. *Spiræaceæ.* De Cand. Prod. Vol. 2, p. 541.

	PURSHIA	De Cand.					
442	tridentata		three toothed	N. America	1826	peat and loam	Pursh. Fl. Am. t. 15.
	Tigarea tridentata Pursh.						
	KERRIA	De Cand.					
443	Japonica	De Cand.	Japan	Japan	1700	com. gard.	Bot. Mag. 1296
	Corchorus Japonicus Thunb. *Spiræa Japonica* Camb.						

No.	Systematic Name.	Authority.	English Name.	Native Country.	Time of Introd.	Soil.	Where figured.
	SPIRÆA	Lin.			Class, ICOSANDRIA. Order, DI—PENTAGYNIA. Lin.		

(Sect. 1. *Ovaries joined at the base, flowers in umbels.*)

No.	Systematic Name.	Authority.	English Name.	Native Country.	Time of Introd.	Soil.	Where figured.
444	opulifolia	Lin.	Opulus leaved	N. America	1690	com. gard.	Duham t. 14

(Sect. 2. *Ovaries not joined at the base, flowers in umbels or cymes.*)

No.	Systematic Name.	Authority.	English Name.	Native Country.	Time of Introd.	Soil.	Where figured.
445	ulmifolia	Scop.	Elm leaved	Siberia	1790	......	Bot. Cab. 1042
	Chamædrifolia	Jacq. (non Lin.)					
446	flexuosa	Fisch.	flexuous	Europe	1820	......	
	Alpina	Hort. (non Pall.)					
447	bella	Sims.	pretty	Nepaul	1820	......	Bot. Mag. 2420
448	vaccinifolia	D. Don.	Whortleberry lvd.	......	1820	peat and loam	Bot. Cab. 1403
449	inflexa	L. C.	inflexed		1829	com. gard.	
450	chamædrifolia	Lin.	Germander lvd.	N. Europe	1789	......	Pall. Fl. Ross. 1, 15
451	trilobata	Lin.	three lobed	Altai Mts.	1801	......	Wat. Den. Br. 68
452	alpina	Pall.	alpine	Siberia	1806	......	Pall. Fl. Ross. 1, 20
453	thalictroides	Pall.	Thalictrum like	Dahuria	1816	......	Pall. Fl. Ross. 1, 20
454	Tobolskia	Lod.	Tobolsk	Russia	1823	......	
455	Hypericifolia	De Cand.	Hypericum lvd.	Europe	1640	......	Schm. Arb. 26
456	3 acutifolia	Willd.	acute leaved			......	
	Sibirica	Hort.					
457	4 crenata	Lin.	crenate leaved		1739	......	
	crenata Ser. (non Bess.)	*obovata* Waldst. et Kit.					
458	corymbosa	Rafin.	corymbose	Virginia	1819	......	Bot. Cab. 671

(Sect. 3. *Ovaries not joined at the base. Flowers in panicles.*)

No.	Systematic Name.	Authority.	English Name.	Native Country.	Time of Introd.	Soil.	Where figured.
459	Betulæfolia	Pall.	Birch leaved	Siberia	1812	......	Wat. Den. Br. 67
	corymbosa Rafin. in Desv. journ. Bot.	*crataegifolia* Link.					
460	lævigata	Lin.	smooth leaved	......	1774	......	Schm. Arb. 1, 49
	Altaicensis	Laxm.					
461	salicifolia	Lin.	Willow leaved	Britain		......	Eng. Bot. 1468
462	1 minor		smaller			......	
463	4 latifolia	Ait.	broad leaved			......	
	carpinifolia Willd.	*obovata* Rafin.					
464	Canadensis	L. C.	Canadian	N. America	1828	......	
465	incarnata	L. C.	flesh coloured		1827	......	
466	undulata	L. C.	waved leaved		1829	......	
467	tomentosa	Lin.	tomentose	......	1736	......	Schm. Arb. 51
468	ariæfolia	Sm.	Aria leaved	......		......	
469	Daurica	L. C.	Daurian	Dahuria	1829	......	

(Sect. 4. *Ovaries 5 joined. Flowers in dense panicles.*)

No.	Systematic Name.	Authority.	English Name.	Native Country.	Time of Introd.	Soil.	Where figured.
470	Sorbifolia	Lin.	Sorbus leaved	Siberia	1759	......	Gmel. Fl. Sib. t. 40
	pinnata	Mœnch.					
471	Pikoviensis	Bess. ?	Pikow	Podolia		......	

Tribe V. *Dryadeæ.* Vent.

No.	Systematic Name.	Authority.	English Name.	Native Country.	Time of Introd.	Soil.	Where figured.
	RUBUS	Lin.	Bramble		Class, ICOSANDRIA. Order, POLYGYNIA. Lin.		

(Sect. 1. *Leaves pinnate or ternate.*)

No.	Systematic Name.	Authority.	English Name.	Native Country.	Time of Introd.	Soil.	Where figured.
472	Rosæsolius	Sm.	Rose leaved	Mauritius	1811	peat and loam	Sm. ic. pic. 3, 60
473	suberectus	Anderson	nearly upright	England		com. gard.	Eng. Bot. 2572
474	strigosus	Michx.	starved	N. America		......	
	Pensylvanicus	Poir.					
475	pauciflorus	Wall	few flowered	Nepaul		......	
476	occidentalis	Lin.	occidental	N. America	1696	......	Dil. Elth. 247, 319
477	Idæus	Lin.	Raspberry	Europe		......	Eng. Bot. 2442
	frambæsianus	Lin.					

(Sect. 2. *Leaves palmate, leaflets three to five.*)

No.	Systematic Name.	Authority.	English Name.	Native Country.	Time of Introd.	Soil.	Where figured.
478	cæsius	Lin.	dewberry	......		......	Eng. Bot. 826
479	corylifolius	Sm.	hazel leaved	......		......	Eng. Bot. 827
	nemorosus	Heyne.					
480	1 flor. pleno		double flowered			......	
481	3 glandulosus	Wallr.	glandulous			......	
	glandulosus	Spreng.					
482	virginicus	L. C.	Virginian	N. America	1829	......	
483	macracinus	L. C.	long branched		1829	......	
484	Americanus	L. C.	American	......	1829	......	
485	niger	L. C.	black		1829	......	
486	spectabilis	Pursh.	shewy	......	1827	......	Pursh. Fl. Am. t. 16
	ribifolius	Willd.					Weihe et Nees Rub. 13, t.1
487	plicatus	Weihe & Nees.	folded	Europe		......	[3 & t. 3 b.
488	affinis	Weihe & Nees.	near	......		......	Weihe et Nees Rub. 16 t.
489	fruticosus	Lin.	shrubby	......		......	Eng. Bot. t. 715
490	1 albus		white fruited			......	
491	2 Tauricus		Taurian			......	
492	3 inermis		unarmed			......	
493	4 apiifolius		Parsley leaved			......	
494	5 rubra		red flowered			......	
495	6 rubra pleno		dble. red flowd.			......	
496	7 fol. variegatis		variegated lvd.			......	
497	intermedius	L. C.	intermediate			......	
498	leucostachus	Schleich.	white spiked	Europe		......	

No.	Systematic Name.	Authority.	English Name.	Native Country.	Time of Introd.	Soil.	Where figured
	RUBUS.						
499	Rhamnifolius	Wiche & Nees.	Buckthorn lvd.	......		com. gard.	Wiche et Nees Rub. 20, t. 6
500	nitidus	Wiche & Nees.	shining	......		......	Wiche et Nees Rub. 17, t. 4
501	1 Canadensis	Lin.	Canadian	N. America	1811	......	

(Sect. 3. *Leaves simple lobed.*)

No.	Systematic Name.	Authority.	English Name.	Native Country.	Time of Introd.	Soil.	Where figured
502	odoratus	Lin.	sweet scented	......	1700	......	Bot. Mag. 323
503	Nutkanus	Moc.	Nootka Sound	......	1826	peat and loam	Bot. Reg. 1368
504	montanus	Libert.	mountain	Belgium		com. gard.	
	POTENTILLA	Nest.	Cinque foil				
505	fruticosa	Lin.	shrubby	Europe		......	
506	3 floribunda	Pursh.	bundle flowered	N. America	1811	......	
	tenuifolia	Schlectendahl.					

Tribe VII. *Roseæ.* De Cand. Prod. Vol. ii. p. 596.

No.	Systematic Name.	Authority.	English Name.	Native Country.	Time of Introd.	Soil.	Where figured
	ROSA	Tourn.	Rose				

Class, ICOSANDRIA. Order, POLYGYNIA. Lin.

(Sect. 1. *Styles cohering.*)

No.	Systematic Name.	Authority.	English Name.	Native Country.	Time of Introd.	Soil.	Where figured
507	arvensis	Huds.	Field	Britain		......	Eng. Bot. t. 188
	sylvestris Herm.	*serpens* Ehrh.	*repens* Jacq.				
508	sempervirens	Lin.	evergreen	Europe	1629	......	Bot. Reg. 465
509	multiflora	Thunb.	many flowered	China	1804	......	
510	Rubifolia	Vill.	Bramble lvd.	N. America	1800	......	
511	Grevillii	Hort.	Greville's	China		......	
512	stylosa	Desv.	styled	Britain		......	Eng. Bot. 1895
513	1 collina	Sm.	hill			......	
514	2 systyla	Bast.	clustered styled			......	
	brevistyla leucrochroa Red.						
515	3 Monsoniana	Lindl.	Lady Monson's			......	
	collina Monsoniana Red.						

(Sect. 2. *Styles not cohering.*)

No.	Systematic Name.	Authority.	English Name.	Native Country.	Time of Introd.	Soil.	Where figured
516	Indica	Lin.	Indian	India	1789	......	Law. Ros. 26
517	1 Reevesii	Hort.	Reeves's			......	
518	2 De Lisle's	Hort.	De Lisle's			......	
519	3 major	Hort.	larger			......	
520	5 longifolia	Red et Thore.	long leaved			......	
	longifolia	Willd.					
521	8 semperflorens	Ser.	ever flowering			......	
	Indica Red. et Thore.	*semperflorens*					
522	Banksiæ	Brown	Lady Banks's	China	1807	......	Bot. Reg. 397
523	1 flor. luteâ		yellow flowered			......	
524	bracteata	Wendl.	bracteate	......	1797	......	Vent. cels. 28
	lucida						
525	microphylla	Roxb.	small leaved	East Indies	1823	......	Bot. Reg. 919
526	Berberifolia	Pall.	Berberry leaved	Persia	1790	......	
527	Gallica	Lin.	French			......	
528	pygmæa	Beib.	pygmy	Caucasus	1820	......	Beib. Cent. 1, 2
529	laxa	Retz.	spreading	N. America		......	Lindl. Ros. 3
530	fruticosa	Bess.	shrubby	Vallesia	1817	......	
531	cinnamomea	Lin.	Cinnamon	Europe		......	Eng. Bot. 2388
532	3 Smithiana	Ser.	Smith's			......	
	cinnamomea	Eng. Bot.					
533	Dahurica	Pall.	Dahurica	Siberia	1824	......	
534	Fraxinifolia	Berk.	Ash leaved	Newfoundland		......	Bot. Reg. 458
535	3 L'Heritierana	Ser.	L'Heritier's			......	
	L'Heritierana	Red. et Thore.					
536	acicularis	Lindl.	acicular	Siberia	1805	......	
537	pimpihellifolia	Lin.	Saxifrage lvd.	Europe		......	Eng. Bot. 187
538	1 vulgaris	Ser.	common			......	

spinosissima Lin. *spinosissima* Jacq. *pimpinellifolia fl. multiplici* Red. *chamærodon* Vill.

GARDEN VARIETIES.

No.	Systematic Name.			Soil.
539	Transparent fl. pl.			......
540	Lady Castlecote			......
541	Hector			......
542	Scotia			......
543	Phyllis			......
544	Ajax			......
545	Ægina			......
546	Hecuba			......
547	Herculea			......
548	Princess Elizabeth			......
549	Mrs. Hooker			......
550	Duba			......
551	Aurora			......
552	Lady Lyndock			......
553	Alexandrina			......
554	Artemisis			......
555	Lady Moncr ef			......
556	Lady Compton			......
557	Dido			......

D

No.	Systematic Name.	Authority.	English Name.	Native Country.	Time of Introd.	Soil.	Where figured.
	Rosa.						
558	Countess of Dunmore					com. gard.	
559	1 flor. mag.					......	
560	semi-double					......	
561	Protea					......	
562	sylvia					......	
563	Double Lady					......	
564	Phyllis					......	
565	Phyllipa					......	
566	Countess of Glasgow					......	
567	Aristides					......	
568	Lady Campbell					......	
569	Sappho					......	
570	Lady Banks					......	
571	Erebus					......	
572	7 myriacantha	Ser.	myriad spined	S. France	1820		Lindl. Ros. 10
573	8 Altaica	Red.	Altaian	Altai Mts.	1818	......	Pall. Fl. Ross. t. 75
	Altaica Willd. *pimpinellifolia* Pall. *grandiflora* Lindl. *Siberica* Tratt.						
574	16 involuta	Ser.	involute	Britain		......	Eng. Bot. t. 2068
	involuta Sm. *nivalis* Don. Cat.						
575	Alpina	Lin.	Alpine	Switzerland	1683	......	Bot. Reg t. 424
576	8 rubella	Ser.	reddish	England		......	Eng. Bot. t. 2521
	rubella Sm. *Candolleana elegans* Thore.						
577	ochroleuca	Swtz.	yellowish flower'd	Siberia		......	
578	canina	Lin.	Dog	Britain		......	Eng. Bot. 992
579	1 glabra	Desv.	smooth			......	
	canina Sm. *sarmentosa* Swtz. *balsamica* Willd. *calycina* Beib.						
580	4 leucantha	Lois.	white flowered			......	
	obtusifolia	Desv.					
581	8 nitidula	Bess.	shining			......	
	Friedlanderiana Bess. *humilis* Bess. *pilosiuscula* Desv.						
582	11 dumetorum	Desv.	Thicket			......	Eng. Bot. t. 2579
	dumetorum	Thuil.					
583	2 uncinella	Bess.	small hooked			......	
	affinis Rau. *cæsia* Sm. *canina cæsia* Sm. *canina cæsia* Lindl. *collina* De Cand.						
584	saxatilis	Stev.	rock	Tauria	1820		
585	caucasica	Pall.	Caucasian	Caucasus		......	

(Sect. 3. *Leaves smooth or hairy underneath more or less glandular.*)

No.	Systematic Name.	Authority.	English Name.	Native Country.	Time of Introd.	Soil.	Where figured.
586	Sabini	Woods	Sabini	Britain		......	
	involuta	Winch.					
587	2 Donniana	Lindl.	Don's			......	
588	rubiginosa	Lin.	Sweetbriar	......		......	Eng. Bot. t. 991
589	9 micrantha	De Cand.	small flowered			......	
	parvifolia	Willd.					
590	16 micrantha	Sm.	small flowered			......	Eng. Bot. t. 2490
	micrantha	Lindl.					
591	suaveolens	Rafin.	sweet-smelling	N. America	1800	......	
592	Hibernica	Sm.	Irish	Ireland		......	Eng. Bot. t. 2196
593	tomentosa	Sm.	tomentose	Britain		......	Eng. Bot. t. 990
594	1 dimorpha	Bess.	double formed			......	
	Smithiana	Ser.					
595	centifolia	Lin.	hundred leaved	S. Europe	1590	......	Red. Ros. i. 1
596	Damascena	Mill.	Damascus	Levant	1573	......	Law. Ros. 38
597	floribunda	Stev.	bundle flowered	Tauria		......	
	rubiginosa	Beib.					
598	alba	Lin.	white flowered	Germany ?	1597	......	Law. Ros. 37
599	1 Boreykiana	Bess.	Boreykiers			......	
	vulgaris	Ser.					

Tribe VIII. *Pomaceæ.* Juss. Gen. p. 334.

No.	Systematic Name.	Authority.	English Name.	Native Country.	Time of Introd.	Soil.	Where figured.
	Cratægus	Lindl.	Hawthorn			Class, Icosandria. Order, Di-Pentagynia. Lin.	

(Sect. 1. *Leaves toothed, or nearly entire.*)

No.	Systematic Name.	Authority.	English Name.	Native Country.	Time of Introd.	Soil.	Where figured.
600	Pyracantha	Pers.	Evergreen Thorn	S. Europe	1629	com. gard.	Schm. Arb. 90
	Mespilus Pyracantha Lin.						
601	crus-galli	Lin.	Cocks-spur	N. America	1691	......	Wat. Den. Br. 56
	lucida Wang. *Mespilus lucida* Ehrh.						
602	2 Pyracanthifolia	De Cand.	Pyracanthus lvd.			......	
	lucida	Dum.					
603	3 Salicifolia	Ait.	Willow leaved			......	
604	4 linearis	De Cand.	linear leaved			......	
	Mespilus linearis Desf.						
605	macrocantha	L. C.	large flowered			......	
606	viridis	L. C.	green fruited			......	
607	punctata	Ait.	dotted fruit			......	
	Mespilus cuneifolia Ehrh. *crus-galli* Duroi.						
608	elliptica	Ait.	elliptic leaved	N. America	1765	......	
	Prunifolia	Poir.					
609	Mexicana	Fl. Mex.	Mexican	Mexico	1827	......	
610	Florida	L. C.	Florida	Florida			
611	parvifolia	Ait.	small leaved	N. America	1704		Wat. Den. Br. 65
	Mespilus axillaris Pers. *tomentosa* Poir. *Xanthocarpos* Lin. *Cratægus tomentosa* Lin.						

No.	Systematic Name.	Authority.	English Name.	Native Country.	Time of Introd.	Soil.	Where figured.
	CRATÆGUS.		(Sect. 2. *Leaves variously lobed or cut.*)				
612	Apiifolia	Michx.	Parsley leaved	N. America	1812	com. gard.	
	oxyacantha Walt. (non Lin.)						
613	1 major		larger			......	
614	pyrifolia	Ait.	Pear leaved	......	1765	......	Wat. Den. Br. 65
	leucophlæos Mœnch. *tomentosa* Duroi. *Mespilus calpodendron* Ehrh.						
615	Caroliniana	L. C.	Carolinian	......		......	
616	glandulosa	Willd.	glandular	Siberia	1750	......	Bot. Cab. t. 1012
	sanguinea Pall. *Mespilus rotundifolia* Ehrh. *Pyrus glandulosa* Mœnch.						
617	glandulifera	L. C.	gland bearing			......	
618	spathulata	Michx.	spathulate lvd.	N. America	1806	......	Bot. Cab. 1261
619	coccinea	Lin.	scarlet fruited	......	1683	......	Wat. Den. Br. 62
	Mespilus Æstivalis Walt.						
620	1 maxima		largest			......	
621	viridis	Lin.	green fruited	......	1810	......	
	cerasifera L. C.						
622	cordata	Mill.	heart-shaped lvd.	......	1738	......	Wat. Den. Br. 63
	populifolia Walt. *acerifolia* Poir. *corallina* Herit. *Mespilus acerifolia* Burg.						
623	edulis	L. C.	edible			......	
624	axillaris	L. C.				......	
625	grossulariæfolia	L. C.	Gooseberry lvd.			......	
626	indentata	L. C.	spiniest			......	
627	nigra	Waldst.	black fruited	Hungary	1819	......	Wat. Den. Br. 64
	Mespilus nigra Willd.						
628	stipulacea	L. C.	stipulaceous			......	
629	flava	Ait.	yellow fruited	N. America	1724		Wat. Den. Br. 59
	glandulosa Michx. *Caroliniana* Pers. *viridis* Walt. *Michauxii* Pers. *Mespilus flexispina* Mœnch.						
630	linearis	L. C.	linear leaved			......	
631	fissa	Bosc.	cleft		1810	......	
632	Olivieriana	Bosc.	Oliviers	Asia Minor	1828	......	
633	oxyacantha	Lin.	Com. Hawthorn	Europe		......	Eng. Bot. t. 2504
634	1 flor. pleno		double flowered			......	
635	2 flor. roseâ		rose flowered			......	
636	3 fol. argenteis		silver leaved			......	
637	4 fol. aureis		golden leaved			......	
638	5 fol. incisis		jagged leaved			......	
639	6 pendula		pendulous			......	
640	7 præcox		early			......	
641	8 fructu puniceâ		red fruited			......	
642	9 fructu luteâ		yellow fruited			......	
643	stricta	L. C.	upright branched			......	
644	Eriocarpa	Lindl.	woolly fruited			......	
645	monogyna	Jacq.	one styled	Siberia		......	Pall. Ross. 1, 12
646	heterophylla	Flugg.	various leaved	N. America	1816	......	
	Mespilus Constantinopolitana Hortul.						
647	Azarolus	Lin.	Azarole	S. Europe	1648	......	Bot. Repos. t. 579
	Pyrus Azarolus Scop.						
648	orientalis	Bosc.	Oriental	......	1810	......	
	Mespilus orientalis Poir. *tanacetifolia* Sm. *pinnata* Dum.						
649	Tanacetifolia	Pers.	tansy leaved	Greece		......	
	2 Celsiana	Hort.	Celsus's				
	Taurica	Hort.					
650	odoratissima	Bot. Repos.	sweetest scented	Crimea		......	Bot. Repos. t. 590
651	laciniata	Ucria.	laciniate lvd.	Sicily	1816	......	
652	melanocarpa	Bieb.	black fruited	Tauria	1820	......	
653	Carpathica	L. C.	Carpathian	Carpathian Mts.		......	
654	corallina	Thunb.	Coralline	France		......	
	ERIOBOTRYA	Lindl.	Loquat				
655	Japonica	Lindl.	Japan	Japan	1787	......	
	COTONEASTER	Medik.					
656	vulgaris	Lindl.	common	S Europe	1656	......	Bot. Mag. t. 2430
	Mespilus cotoneaster						
657	tomentosa	Lindl.	woolly leaved	Europe	1759	......	
	Mespilus tomentosa Willd. (non Lam.) *eriocarpa* De Cand.						
658	elliptica		elliptic leaved			......	
659	affinis	Lindl.	allied	Nepaul	1820	......	
	Mespilus integerrima Hamil. *affinis* Don.						
660	acuminata	Lindl.	acuminate lvd.	......	1820	......	Bot. Cab. t. 912
	Mespilus acuminata Lod.						
661	nummularia	Lindl.	moneywort lvd.	......	1824	......	Bot. Cab. t. 1512
662	frigida	Wall.	frigid	......	1824	......	
663	uva-ursi	Lindl.	Bearberry lvd.		1820	loam and peat	
664	microphylla	Lindl.	small leaved		1820	......	Bot. Cab. t. 1374
665	melanocarpa	Fisch.	black fruited	N. America	1700	com. gard.	Bot. Cab. t. 1531
	AMELANCHIER	Medik.					Bot. Mag. t. 2430
666	vulgaris	Mœnch.	common	S. Europe	......		*Cratægus rotundifolia* Lam.
	Mespilus Amelanchier Lin. *Pyrus Amelanchier* Willd. *Aronia rotundifolia* Pers.						Schm. Arb. t. 84
667	Botryapium	De Cand.	Grape Pear	N. America	1746	......	
	Mespilus canadensis Lin. *Cratægus ramosa* Lin. *Pyrus Botryapium* Lin. *Aronia Botryapium* Pers.						

No.	Systematic Name.	Authority.	English Name.	Native Country.	Time of Introd.	Soil.	Where figured.
	CRATÆGUS.						
668	1 ramosa		branched	N. America		com. gard.	
669	2 spicata		spiked			......	
670	sanguinea	De Cand.	bloody	......	1800	......	
	Pyrus sanguinea Pursh. *Aronia sanguinea* Nutt.						
671	ovalis	De Cand.	oval leaved	......	1800	......	
	Cratægus spicata Lam. *Mespilus Amelanchier* Walt. *Pyrus ovalis* Willd.						
	MESPILUS	Lindl.	Medlar				
672	Germanica	Lin.	German	Europe		......	Eng. Bot. t. 152, 3
673	grandiflora	Sm.	large flowered			......	Bot. Mag. t. 3642
	Smithii De Cand. *lobata* Poir.						
674	Caroliniana	L. C.	Carolinian	N. America		......	
674	capitata	L. C.	capitate			......	
	PYRUS	Lin.	Pear				

(Sect. 1. *Fruit more or less turbinate, or somewhat globose, pedicels simple umbellate. Leaves simple glandless.*)

No.	Systematic Name.	Authority.	English Name.	Native Country.	Time of Introd.	Soil.	Where figured.
675	communis	Lin.	common pear	England		......	Eng. Bot. t. 1784
676	1 flor. pleno		double flowered			......	
677	2 fol. variegatis		variegated lvd.			......	
678	Bollwylleriana	De Cand.	Bollwyllers	Germany	1786	......	Bot. Cab. . 1009
	Pollreria	Lin.					
679	vestita		clothed			......	
680	amygdaliformis	Vill.	Almond formed	S. Europe	1810	......	
	communis Gouan. (non Lin.) *salicifolia* Balb.						
681	salicifolia	Lin.	Willow leaved	Russia	1780	......	Bot. Reg. t. 514
682	1 spuria	Hort.	spurious			......	
683	Sinaica	Thouin.	Mount Sinai	Levant	1820	......	Wat. Den. Br. t. 9
	orientalis	Hort.					
684	1 undulata	Hort.	waved leaved			......	
685	nivalis	Lin.	snowy	S. Europe		......	......

(Sect. 2. *Fruit globular, or more frequently depressed globular, pedicels simple umbellate. Leaves simple glandless.*)

No.	Systematic Name.	Authority.	English Name.	Native Country.	Time of Introd.	Soil.	Where figured.
686	præcox	Swt.	early	Russia	1784	......	
687	dioica	Willd.	diœcious		1811	......	
	apetala	Munchh.					
688	spectabilis	Ait.	shewy	China	1780	......	Bot. Mag. t. 267
689	prunifolia	Willd.	Plum leaved	Siberia	1758	......	Mill. ic. 2. 269
	Malus spectabilis Desf. *sinensis* Dum.						
690	1 hyemalis	L. C.	winter			......	
691	2 Siberica	L. C.	Siberian			......	
692	baccata	Lin.	berried	......	1784	......	Wat. Den. Br. t. 51
	Malus baccata Desf.						
693	Coronaria	Lin.	Crown	Virginia	1724	......	Bot. Mag t. 2009
694	angustifolia	Ait.	narrow leaved	N. America	1750	......	Wat. Den. Br. t. 132
	Coronaria Waghm. (non Ait.) *sempervirens* Desf. *malus sempervirens* Poir.						

(Sect. 3. *Fruit globose, flowers in racemose-corymbs. Leaves simple glandless, underneath cottony.*)

No.	Systematic Name.	Authority.	English Name.	Native Country.	Time of Introd.	Soil.	Where figured.
695	Aria	Ehrh.	White Beam Tree	Britain		......	Eng. Bot. t. 1858
	Mespilus aria Scop. *Sorbus aria* Crantz.						
696	1 dentata	Lod.				......	
697	intermedia	Ehrh.	intermediate	Sweden	1789	......	Flor. Dan. t. 401
	Cratægus scandica Wahlenb. *Sorbus intermedia* Pers.						
698	1 latifolia	De Cand.	broad leaved			......	
	Cratægus latifolia Poir. *Sorbus latifolia* Pers. *Cratægus dentata* Thuil.						
699	Polonica	L. C.	Poland			......	

(Sect. 4. *Fruit globose or turbinate, Leaves pinnate, with an odd one. Flowers corymbose, pedicels branched.*)

No.	Systematic Name.	Authority.	English Name.	Native Country.	Time of Introd.	Soil.	Where figured.
700	pinnatifida	Sm.	pinnatifid lvd.	England		......	Eng. Bot. t. 2331
	Sorbus hybrida Sm. *Pyrus hybrida* Sm. Fl. Brit. (non Willd.)						
701	1 pendula	Hort.	pendulous			......	
	aucuparia	Gært.	mountain Ash	Britain			Eng. Bot. t. 337
	Sorbus aucuparia Lin. *Mespilus aucuparia* All.						
702	1 fol. variegatis	L. C.	variegated lvd.			......	
703	Americana	De Cand.	American	Canada	1782	......	Wat. Den. Br. t. 54
	Sorbus Americana Pursh.						
704	Sorbus	Gært.	True Service Tree	England		......	Eng. Bot. t. 350
	Sorbus domestica Lin. *Pyrus domestica* Sm. Eng. Bot.						
705	1 maliformis	Hort.	apple formed			......	
706	lanuginosa	De Cand.	woolly	Hungary	1820	......	
	Sorbus lanuginosa Kit.						
707	spuria	De Cand.	spurious		1800	......	
	Sorbus spuria Pers. *Mespilus sorbifolia* Poir. *Pyrus hybrida* Mœnch.						
708	1 glabra	L. C.	smooth			......	
709	2 rubra	L. C.	red			......	

(Sect. 5. *Fruit globose, Leaves simple, bearing glands about the leaf-stalk. Flowers corymbose.*)

No.	Systematic Name.	Authority.	English Name.	Native Country.	Time of Introd.	Soil.	Where figured.
710	Nepalensis	L. C.	Napaul			......	
711	Xanthocarpa	Hort.	yellow fruited			......	
712	melanocarpa	Willd.	black fruited	N. America	1700	......	Schm. Arb. t. 86
	Aronia arbutifolia Pers.						
713	Arbutifolia	Lin.	Arbutus leaved	......	1700	......	Mill. ic. t. 10
	Cratægus pyrifolia Lam. *Aronia pyrifolia* Pers. *Cratægus serrata* Poir. *Mespilus arbutifolia* Sm.						

Indexes

Index of plant names

Names without comment have been verified as correct. Incorrect names are followed by the correct modern equivalents, for example: *Picea pinsapo* = *Abies pinsapo*. The correct modern names are also indexed, with the older names in parentheses, for example: *Abies pinsapo* (as *Picea pinsapo*).

Doubt as to the exact equivalence of a name is indicated by a question mark. Where there is much doubt the phrase (application uncertain) is used. Where names cannot be found in *Index Kewensis* and thus are presumably not validly published, the phrase (name cannot be traced) is added.

Cultivar names in the Catalogue of Plants (1836) are not generally indexed.

139

141

Index of Plant Names

143

144

145

General index

Entries in bold type refer to illustrations.